FROM PLANET ORK TO THE STARS...

Perhaps most famous for his characterization of the friendly space visitor in TV's "Mork and Mindy" show, Robin Williams officially made the transition to superstar when he was nominated for an Academy Award for "Good Morning Vietnam" in 1988. But this transformation was neither sudden nor easy. Devoting many years to performing live before enthralled audiences, Robin led a stormy personal and professional life.

Now, Marianne Robin-Tani invites you backstage to share the successes and failures of this supremely talented artist. Here is the entire story of an inspired, eccentric comic actor whose humor and startling spontaneity seem from out of this world. From his box-office flops and separation from his wife to his sold-out performances and bright prospects for the future, here is an unforgettable, up-close-and-personal look at one of America's most brilliant stars.

ROBIN WILLIAMS

Marianne Robin Tani

ST. MARTIN'S PRESS/NEW YORK

Library of Congress Catalog Card Number: 87-063542

ISBN: 0-312-91023-1 Can. ISBN: 0-312-91025-8

Printed in the United States of America

First St. Martin's Press mass market edition/August 1988

10 9 8 7 6 5 4 3 2 1

TO:

Kathy—a rotten big sister at twelve, who became my soulmate, support system, and closest friend (and my cute, talented brother-in-law, Scott);

Annie and Jake—who provided me with an earth, moon, and stars filled with the love and wisdom only grandparents can give;

And Velcro—who stuck with me through thick and thin.

The author would like to sincerely thank the following for their infinite assistance and forbearance:

Yoko Asano, Hether Churchill, El Camino College Library, Tom Green, Janna Wong-Healy, Sandy and Reggie Holmes, Bruce Johnson, Los Angeles County Public Library System, Anne Lowenkopf, Sheldon Lowenkopf, Paul Miranne, Tom Mitter, Madeleine Morel, Pennee and Archie Robin, Joni Roundtree, Kaz and Jenny Sakamoto, David D. Shumacher, Cynthia Takano, Noriyasu Tani, Richard Taylor, The Academy of Motion Picture Arts & Sciences Library, the Toji family, UCLA Theater Arts Library, and Dennis Umeda.

1

A Leprechaun in Detroit

EVERY CLASS HAS ONE—THE FAT LITTLE KID WHO GETS picked on and called names. At Gorton Elementary School in suburban Lake Forest, Illinois, during the late 1950s, the little boy everyone loved to hate was Robin Williams.

"Most of the kids were bigger than me, and they wanted to prove they were bigger by throwing me into walls," Robin said.

Born in Chicago on July 21, 1952, to Robert and Laurie Williams, a couple he would describe as "George Burns and Gracie Allen looking like Alistair Cooke and Audrey Hepburn," Robin's tough time at school was partly a result of his dad's job as a troubleshooter for Ford's Lincoln-Continental division. Company transfers meant that the family had to make frequent moves between Detroit and Chicago, and Robin attended six different schools during one eight-year period. And having a name your father picked out of a children's book—a name that's the same as the red, red, bird that goes bob-bob-bobbing along—didn't help Robin move quickly up the macho social scale, either. Being named Larry or Kevin would have probably reduced the malicious teasing to a more manageable level.

Robin has remembered himself as a friendless, pudgy kid whose nicknames were "Dwarf" and "Leprechaun." Although loyal mom Laurie has vehemently denied that her son was ever overweight, Robin has insisted that he began telling jokes as a way to keep "from getting the shit kicked out of me."

Because of the frequent moves, he was continually the new kid in town, and since he was virtually an only child, he didn't have a built-in support group of brothers or sisters to help shield him from the cruelty of the farm kids or the children of auto-assembly factory workers at the public schools he attended.*

---

*The union of Robin's parents was a second marriage for both of them, and each had a son in their previous marriages. Robin's half-brothers, Todd and Loren, were seven and nineteen years older, respectively, and he didn't meet them until he was about ten. He claims that Todd—to the fury of his mother—would come into Robin's room and demand that the younger boy empty out his piggy bank to supply his half-brother with beer money.

His attempts to avoid the bullies he knew were lying in wait for him at school were in vain. At one point, he even wished he could find a way to go in through the roof. He did what he could to joke his way out of these confrontations, but being a new *rich* kid only made matters worse. His family wasn't ultra-wealthy, but Robin has joked that the troublemakers guessed he was well-off when he'd ask them to join his lacrosse team (adding that the guys always thought lacrosse was an object found in la church).

After a few years of this torture, Robin's family moved into the exclusive Detroit suburb of Bloomfield Hills and enrolled him in a private school. At first, life at Detroit Country Day School was only marginally more tolerable—instead of returning home with cuts and bruises from beatings, Robin would have his ego battered by academic bullies. "All these hyperintellectuals would really lay into me with lines like, 'That was a very asinine thing to say, Williams,' " he said.

Robin quickly made himself a model student, proudly donning the school's regulation uniform of blazer, striped tie, and slacks. He carried his books in a briefcase and wore his light brown hair parted on the side and neatly combed back off his forehead.

Since Detroit Country was an all-boys school, getting acquainted with members of the opposite sex posed considerable logistical problems. Robin had only fleeting contact with girls, when busloads of them were brought in from a nearby all-girls school to be presented at dances.

Fighting their shyness and embarrassment and eager for what contact they could grab during these all-too-brief meetings, the boys tried hard to ignore the chaperones lining the crèpe-paper-strewn gym walls and the unreality of the awkward situation they'd been thrust into. Just about the time they were wondering if they'd finally encountered a few friendly girls, the young ladies were unceremoniously trooped back onto the bus. Once, Robin found himself chasing it down the driveway, yelling at them to come back and show him how they used all those *things* they had on them.

Robin has claimed that his school's motto was "Monsanto incorpori glorius maxima copia" (Latin for "When the going gets tough, the tough go shopping"). Faculty members were dedicated to teaching students the poise and confidence they would need to become corporate executives and civic leaders. One such exercise during the ninth grade required that all the boys give a speech at lunchtime. Robin did a comedy speech which was well-received, but included a Polish joke. Only when he returned to his seat did he discover that the school's stout assistant headmaster was of Polish descent, and Robin was in deep trouble. Evidently he survived it.

Tired of being the underdog during his first year of high school, Robin decided to gain control of the situation by changing his flab into muscle. By sticking to a rigid diet and a vigorous exercise routine, including hours of calisthenics every day, he lost thirty pounds in a year. Down to a fighting weight of 103 pounds, Robin made the wrestling team.

Undefeated in his freshman year, Robin was feeling like a big shot as he entered the state finals—only to find himself mismatched against a huge, balding guy from upstate Michigan who looked as if he was eight years older than the other students. Twisted up like a pretzel, parts of Robin's body were pushed into places he'd never believed humanly possible. He ended up with a dislocated shoulder.

After being forced to give up wrestling in his sophomore year, Robin then discovered the joys of football. Assigned to the position of safety, he found that a 103-pound safety has an extremely difficult time stopping a 200-pound running back. He was knocked over by every offensive play in the book, and at last asked the coach to paint him white so he could camouflage himself as a yard marker. After a week, he was off the team.

Soccer was the next team sport Robin attempted. He thought it was a great sport because it requires neither excessive brawn nor height—physical qualities Robin seriously lacked—to be an accomplished player. His natural agility saved him from being crushed as he zipped between players, kicking the ball across the field.

Sadly, although Robin achieved varsity letters in three sports and knocked himself out playing just about every other game imaginable, his busy dad never found the time to watch his matches. Mark Schlegel, the headmaster's son at Detroit Country Day School, thought Robin's father was either dead or had gotten a divorce because he never came to any of the sporting events.

Being on athletic teams helped to round out Robin's personality and he finally made many friends. Most of his pals in high school were Jewish (he attended fourteen *bar mitzvahs* in one year). His chums even made him an honorary Jew and told people he attended services at Temple Beth Dublin.

Yet prior to his high school rounding-out, young Mr. Williams had been an extremely lonely little rich boy, and for a period lived in a thirty-room house set on twenty acres of land. He has emphasized that his family wasn't *that* rich—the house was rented and they didn't heat all the rooms. But no other kids lived in the neighborhood, so Robin's sole occasional playmate was the maid's son.

He turned the house's attic into his private retreat, a wonderful imaginary land filled with the objects of his childhood passion—10,000 toy soldiers. He kept them carefully sorted in boxes divided up by historical periods and adored staging elaborate full-scale battles where Confederate soldiers were fending off GIs using automatic weapons and tanks, while Nazis were sending sword-wielding knights of the Round Table off to concentration camps. He even had a 10′ × 3′ board covered with sand that he made into a model of Guadalcanal. Of course, he acted out all the roles himself.

"I had to use all these voices and sound effects with my standing army—there were incredible wars where I took no prisoners [and created] actual burnings of villages, like Kublai Khan," he recalled.

Carl, his pet turtle, was crowned king of a castle Robin built and was the supreme commander of these time-warped skirmishes. One day, Robin decided that letting Carl go free would make the small reptile happier than reigning supreme in the attic, and he flushed the unfortunate beast down the toilet.

After that, Robin was left with his dog Duke, a sweet animal just a wee bit short on intellect. When the boy and his canine played hide and seek, Duke seemed to think that if he couldn't see Robin, then he himself couldn't be spotted. His enthusiasm for the game was his downfall; Robin would track Duke down by zeroing in on the loud thumps made by the dog's tail cheerfully smacking the parquet floor.

Robin continued to study military tactics, fascinated by the intricacies of the maneuvers. Then one day "my father sat me down and explained what war was all about," he said. "I was about ten years old at the time and it scared me."

The attic hideaway was also where Robin's first informal training in standup comedy took place. Over and over again he would listen to tape-recorded televised comedy routines and records by his idol, Jonathan Winters, then practice telling jokes for hours on end. "I think my own imagination was my best friend, my true companion. It let me make up characters I could talk to—characters I could become," he claimed.

Robin's vivid imagination was about the only wild thing about him during his childhood. He was extremely straitlaced and polite in public, always calling adults, including his parents, "Sir" and "Ma'am."

Nelia Hopkins, a classmate from Gorton Elementary School, remembered how Robin was "stiff and formal, like cardboard, walking around reserved and straight-backed like a small military officer." Another schoolmate, Robert Young, said: "Most of the time he was a little Mr. Super Straight ... a bit on the quiet side and real dull."

Sometimes, Robin would become so withdrawn that he'd tune into an interior fantasy world filled with different people speaking in strange voices. School chum Thom Goldberg recalled one time when Robin was running in a track meet and the "spectators were suddenly amazed to hear a weird collection of voices. There was a high-pitched woman's voice, then a deeper-pitched man's voice responding." They even heard an old person with a foreign accent speaking to a younger person with a completely different accent. Everyone burst out laughing when they realized the zany conversations were all coming from Robin, unself-consciously running around the track all by himself.

Valerie Velardi, Robin's wife, has agreed that growing up alone caused the comedian to create his own world, and this has sometimes isolated him from the "real" world. "He has a very rich private life, and it's hard to filter in," she said. "It's hard to get in deep with someone who's used to taking care of himself only."

Robin has said that he gets his wacky energy from his mother, a woman he's often referred to as "a crazy Southern belle. She always wanted to go into show business." A lively and buoyant woman, Robin's mom taught him early on to appreciate off-the-wall humor. When Robin was still a little tyke, Laurie recited poems such as: "Spider crawling on the wall/Ain't you got no sense at all?/Don't you know that wall's been plastered?/Get off that wall, you little spider." Her favorite one was: "I love you in red/I love you in blue/But most of all/I love you in blue." He swore that his mom owned a book written by a nineteenth century English princess—well-known for the glamorous parties she threw—entitled *Balls I Have Held.*

"Lord Posh" is Robin's nickname for his father, whom he has likened to "an elegant man, like the lord governor general of India" with an amusing but droll sense of humor. Since Robert was nearly fifty when Robin was born, the comedian was raised in a double-generation gap situation by a father old enough to be his grandfather.

However lonely he was in his younger years, Robin always insisted that he wasn't unhappy and that his parents gave him plenty of love. He remembered that Christmas as an only child was a "super, super-special time. I knew all the goodies were saved for me." The snow in Michigan cloaked the world in white magic and he believed in Santa Claus until he was nine and chanced to see his father sneaking the presents downstairs. Never one to be disappointed for long, Robin decided he didn't care where the presents came from as long as he still got them all.

And so life had evened out by the end of his junior year in high school—Robin was a member of the *magna cum laude* society and expected to be the president of his senior class. His future intentions consisted of a Midwesterner's dream idea of WASPish American success: entrance in a solid ivy-league or Midwestern college, possibly a career in the foreign service, and marriage to a nice woman (once he managed to overcome his shyness enough to begin dating).

However, just before his senior year, Robert Williams retired from the Ford Motor Company, and made a move destined to change the scope and fabric of Robin's life forever.

2

Stranger in Some Strange Lands

JUST WHAT IN THE WORLD WAS THAT WEIRD GREY glop rolling in over the hills? Clouds of poison gas?

Seventeen-year-old Robin was in the back seat of his parents' car heading towards San Francisco during the summer of 1969. His father had decided to pull up the family's Midwestern stakes and live out his retirement years in the pastoral splendor of Tiburon, a small town in Marin County, just north of the City on the Bay.

As the car sped into the whitish-grey clouds, Robert was forced to put on the car's lights and turn on the windshield wipers. The sunny day grew dim, and it became almost impossible to see beyond the car's hood. Robin had never seen weather like this before and it was frightening. It was not the best of introductions to California.

Robin's initial encounter with fog was only

the first of many bizarre things he'd find on the West Coast. The vast differences between the Golden State of Consciousness (especially places even remotely close to San Francisco) during the last year of the swinging sixties and the staid conservatism of Middle America would be enough to send anyone into a frenzy, wondering "Where the hell am I?" "In terms of cultural shock, it probably would have been easier for me to move to Mexico. I had total cultural shock," he said.

Although the weird atmospheric conditions first alerted Robin that this place was going to be unusual, nothing on earth could have prepared him for the shock that was to hit him on his first day of school. Neatly groomed, his short hair carefully slicked back into place, Robin entered Redwood High School wearing a tasteful suit and tie and carrying his books in a briefcase. The other kids, dressed in tattered blue jeans, tie-dyed tee shirts, and long, patchwork granny dresses wondered who the nerd was. Schoolmate Philip Russell remembered thinking that this new character must be from outer space.

Robin described how bizarre the situation was for him as well: "Coming from the tightness and discipline of an all-boys private school and all of a sudden—bang!—the kids were going, 'Look, Tommy, the walls are melting.' Everyone was on acid and they had gestalt history classes." Back in Detroit he had been required to wear a tie, but at Redwood "even socks were optional."

Although he may have started off as an alien, Robin soon found that he was no longer a round peg in a square world. His own brand of happy madness fell right into place with the groovy, do-your-own-thing counterculture that was spreading like an amoeba among the youth of America.

Arriving in Marin was what made Robin blossom. "It was my senior year in high school and all that subliminal stuff that had been building up in me began to emerge, all those characters and sounds," he said. "That was when something kind of snapped in me, and I began to suspect that I was funny."

The entire transformation took a few months. Robin kept wearing a tie and carrying his briefcase for a few weeks, attempting to ignore murmurings he heard about how his unmellow straight attitude was destroying the school's karma.

Finally cracking under peer pressure, Robin wore jeans one day. To celebrate his newfound freedom, a friend gave him a Hawaiian shirt, which resulted in Robin joyously diving wholeheartedly into the wonderful world of freakdom and free love. He began to grow his hair long, and soon fit right in. "Someone gave him a Hawaiian shirt," his mother said, "and suddenly there were girls."

Redwood High's curriculum offered a full range of life-experience and mind-expanding classes, including pop psychology and filmmaking. The school also had a complete black studies department, even though there was only one black kid at the school. Teachers would hold encounter-group sessions involving hug therapy during class time, and one teacher would occasionally stop what he was doing to let a few students beat out percussion rhythms on their desks while the rest did wild dances around the room.

Like all good counterculture kids of the era, Robin experimented with different types of mind-altering substances, most of which he found didn't agree with him. Cannabis sativa—something he had never even glimpsed in Detroit—only made him sleepy and paranoid. One friend gave him peyote (without informing Robin what he was ingesting), and sent him off onto a bad trip. Robin remembered his friend's face melting away and expanding like Silly Putty—an experience he wasn't too keen to repeat.

Another force kept Robin from getting too involved in chemical-induced mind expansion: He was on the cross-country running team and thought smoking dope would throw off his training. His hero was Frank Shorter (later a winner of the Olympic marathon), and Robin even grew a mustache to emulate him. Best friend Phil Russell took on the fantasy role of Shorter's cross-country teammate, and the two buddies would train for hours, running across the beautiful, rolling green hills of Marin.

Once, when Robin did give in to his mates and smoke some grass before running—against his better judgment—he came up a hill and encountered one of Marin's many huge turkey vultures. Certain the bird would flee from the charging boys, Robin ran right up to it. Surprise: The bird held its ground, hissed menacingly, and flapped its enormous wings in Robin's face. Pale and cringing, and certain that such a horrible experience would happen again if he ran stoned, Robin vowed never to mix smoking and running again.

Another training session sent the team up a gorgeous trail high on Mt. Tamalpais, and Robin remembered coming upon a sloping cliff, framed by fog, overlooking Stinson Beach. He felt a Buddhist oneness with the world; ignoring the shouted warnings of his chums, he gave in to the beautiful temptation of the moment and ran straight down the hill and into the water. Of course, his legs—which had just been dragged over mountain trails for an hour—saw the moment quite differently. They cramped up so badly from the freezing shock that Robin nearly had to crawl back to school.

Among the few things on the West Coast that didn't seem totally bizarre to Robin were the famous California girls, but even they were . . . well, different. Back in the Midwest, teenagers were still adhering to more conservative-type dating: borrow dad's car, drive to a girl's home, politely greet her folks, then take your date out for a movie and burger. In Marin, free love was the name of the game, and the rules and traditions surrounding mating went up in the smoke of the sexual revolution.

One thing that still held true, however—even for wild, liberated hippies—was a desperate need for pocket money. No different from his peers on this count, Robin took a job at the Trident Restaurant in the nearby town of Sausalito.

Now a completely sanitized tourist attraction—sort of a Disney-meets-the-Beatniks scenario—Sausalito in the late sixties was still a hip artist colony. The quaint wooden-framed houses lining the sparkling bay were painted a rainbow of different colors, and the galleries featured everything from pop art to landscapes.

In Robin's opinion, the waitresses at the Trident were both the most gorgeous and the strangest women on the planet. Applying for the job was closer to auditioning; the women even had to have their pictures taken.

Most of these flower children would wear exotic costumes to work, such as macraméd halter tops with holes large enough for tender parts of the waitresses' breasts to poke through. Thinking he was doing then a favor, Robin would point out the protruding bits of anatomy, but the girls would hush him, explaining that they were merely trying for bigger tips. After all, people were "sisters" and "brothers" in those days, and sharing one's body was a completely natural and healthy thing to do.

The Trident was an earthy health-food restaurant where the foods served seemed to be brimming with vibrant energy. Robin had heard all about organic chemistry back in Middle America, but organic food was definitely a new one. His first experience with wheatberry bread made him wonder if he wasn't chewing on roofing tiles, and he thought *mu* tea was somehow extracted from a cow's bowels.

Completely enveloped in this wondrous new lifestyle, Robin still had one shred of Midwestern conservatism he hadn't rid himself of—his chosen career. After graduating from high school and being accepted at Claremont Men's College in southern California, he picked political science as his major in preparation for his life to come in the foreign service. In a few short years, Robin's work would, indeed, require travel all over the world, but it wouldn't be in the capacity of an embassy attaché. The delicate balance of Robin's future life was completely altered by one of the eight classes he took during his freshman year—an elective in theater. "After my first day, I was hooked," he recalled.

The members of his class formed an improvisation group called The Synergy Trust, and they played to a packed house in the school's eighty-seat theater every Friday night. Robin was having the time of his life—to such a degree that he didn't bother going to any other classes and subsequently flunked out.

The beginning of the 1971–72 school year found him back in the Bay Area, studying theater at Marin Junior College. Determined to make it before the footlights, Robin took his studies seriously. He was particularly attracted to a Shakespearean drama class that rehearsed and performed the Elizabethan plays in a replica of the original Globe Theatre stage.

While his father told him to keep an alternate career in mind—just in case, (and even suggested that his son take up welding)—Robin's mother was tickled that someone in the family was going to try to make it in show business. Laurie was sure that Robin's maternal grandmother (a fun-loving lady who adored watching men's wrestling matches) would be immeasurably proud.

The ecstasy of acting was only topped by one event that year. Robin fell in love for the first time, with a gentle beauty who had long blonde hair the color of sun-kissed honey. He wrote reams of poetry to her, and sometimes showed them to his mother before bestowing them on his love. Laurie remembered telling him that the poems didn't rhyme, but Robin patiently explained that they were a stream of consciousness like a river flowing to the sea, that needs not the rigidity of the tides. Shaking her head at her son's obvious infatuation, Laurie offered him the use of her car, but Robin only sped off, trilling that his heart had such wings, he would soar over the clouds to his love's home. The romance was not meant to be forever, unfortunately.

For the next two-and-a-half years, he worked hard at his craft, and then heard an announcement so exciting it caused his heart to do cartwheels. The famous Juilliard School of Art had just started an acting department and was searching for talent across the country.

Since every actor in his right mind has dreams of making it big on Broadway, and also because Robin wanted to prove to his doubting dad that he could make it (who seemed to feel that any accomplishments outside of mainstream America couldn't amount to much success), he went to San Francisco to audition for a scholarship.

The chances of getting one seemed slim. The recruiters, out from New York, were seeing an average of fifty people a day. Seeing how good the others were, Robin felt his self-confidence faltering. He had no idea what they were looking for in a student, and wondered if he had enough talent. Yet repeating over and over to himself all the good things his professors and classmates had ever said to him and reliving those great sessions of side-splitting improvisation in the packed theater at Claremont helped to buoy him up.

When his name was finally called, he gathered up every shred of confidence he had before striding onto the stage and beginning Malvolio's speech from *Twelfth Night*. Next he let it all hang out, and went off the deep end as crazy Leper Lepellier from *A Separate Peace*. The judges must have liked what they saw, because this quintessential California hippie, who had so recently been a Midwestern preppie, soon found himself walking through Juilliard.

Once again, Robin found himself thrown into an alien culture. Beach parties and cool Redwood forests suddenly gave way to bumping crowds and sooty high rises. Dressed in his bright Hawaiian shirt, baggy cotton pants that tied at the ankle, and rubber flip-flops, Robin was every New Yorker's idea of a hopeless California weirdo, circa late 1973.

Back on the other coast, he'd known women who would shed tears of sorrow over the necessity of swatting a housefly; imagine how appalled Robin felt riding on a bus one day when an old man had a heart attack and keeled over. Nobody else wanted to help or even acted as if it mattered.

After the initial jolting contrast of cities lost some of its impact, Robin was enticed by the excitement and energy that has always driven New York. He prowled the streets, observing all the ethnic diversities and storing them for future reference. With a group of friends, he did mime in whiteface on the steps of the Metropolitan Museum of Art, and sometimes collected $150 for his efforts. He lost himself in the galleries and museums; investigated all the magnificent, out-of-the-way, and cheap restaurants; and absorbed as much theater as he possibly could. He sidestepped drag queens as well as thugs clad in black leather jackets. The city really toughened him. He said moving to the Big Apple at that point in his life was a fantastic experience, because he'd "been in danger of becoming terminally mellow and it peeled away that layer very quickly."

Even the methods of teaching at Juilliard were completely unlike any he'd experienced so far.

In his previous classes, the students performed scenes and then dissected them in long debates. Teachers had been quick to praise and point out what had worked well. Juilliard was more like entering the Marine Corps. First the students were made to feel like worthless, no-talent pieces of dog meat, and then they were taught all the various and sundry techniques they would need as actors.

Robin found out post haste that he was walking too quickly, his enunciation was lousy, and no one beyond the first few rows could hear him. After performing Dudley Moore's religious monologue from *Beyond the Fringe,* his teacher gave him an ultimatum—either prepare the entire piece again with inflections and feelings that would make it Robin's interpretation rather than just a regurgitation, or completely forget about attempting a career on the stage.

Everything about the school was intense. The demanding schedule of acting, movement, speech, and even fencing classes required that the students be at school from 8:00 in the morning until 9:00 or 10:00 at night. Just as the Juilliard School of Music concentrated on classical music, the acting school was completely geared towards work on the classical stage.*

---

*One of Robin's fondest recollections about Juilliard is a speech given by the school's principal, John Houseman, emphasizing that live theater was hungrily awaiting their

Robin's saving grace during this rough period was his friendship with another advanced student who had come from Cornell, Christopher Reeve. They only lived about five blocks from each other and found many days of solace in each other's company. They read lines and rehearsed scenes together, sat on the roof drinking cheap wine and philosophizing about love, and did everything friends do to help each other over the rough spots of growing up while training for careers in a field everyone tells you is impossible to break into.

Reeve remembered his initial glimpses of Robin around school: "At first he wasn't comfortable in New York. He was a California kid who wore karate clothes and a beret and was out of sync with people." Another fellow student said Robin was "the kind of student who kept his eyes and ears open and his mouth shut. Nobody had any inkling that he would be such a big star."

Determined to be independent, Robin turned down his father's offer of a plane ticket home

---

fresh blood, and begging them not to be swayed by the celluloid temptations of television or the movies. A week later Houseman was seen in a Volvo commercial and a few years after that he starred in a TV series called *The Paper Chase.*

for his first Christmas vacation. It was his first holiday season away from his family and the first snowy one in many years. The freezing wind seemed to cut right through his bones and even putting on the radiator full blast wouldn't warm up his tiny apartment. Everything seemed devastatingly cold—the weather, the unfeeling New Yorkers, even the bleak dim sunlight.

Day after day Robin walked the streets, seeking some inkling of warmth, but the faces he passed held no compassion. His own family and friends seemed light-years away. The happy people he saw shopping and admiring the Christmas decorations only pushed him deeper into despair.

Then came a morning when he was too depressed even to leave his apartment. Everything seemed devoid of color and life. His studies and books held no interest; nor did music, drink, or food. Overwhelmed by loneliness, he gave in to the crushing weight and broke down. For two days, he lost total control of himself and wallowed in his misery. The black spell ended only after he realized that there was no place lower for him to go—he had to pull himself back together or else go totally off the deep end.

With that realization, a calmness and peace began washing over him, cleaning out the spaces that had so recently been filled with the poison of self-pity. Robin was back in charge of himself. He knew he was stronger, and that he could go on to accomplish anything he wanted.

This newfound vigor flowed through his veins, and Robin plunged back into his classes and worked his tail off to become the best actor he could.

3

Robin Finds True Love at the Zoo

THE REMAINDER OF ROBIN'S FIRST YEAR IN NEW York flew by. The next year also passed quickly—and enjoyably—thanks to a sweet new companion.

Robin learned that a young woman he had known back home was now living in New York, and the two transplanted Californians soon became fast friends. It was wonderful to have someone to hang out with, someone who shared his delight at the foibles of New Yorkers and enjoyed exploring the hidden corners of this amazing city.

His new friend was so ethereal, however, that Robin often found himself chasing her around, worried out of his mind that she would end up in a back alley with her throat slashed. She thought nothing of traipsing through the worst neighborhoods clad only in a frothy, white lace dress. Constantly scolding her to be more careful, Robin would surreptitiously follow her, praying that no distress would befall his damsel.

The girl only shushed him. A trusting soul, she insisted that one gets back what one gives out in life; meaning that if she loved others, they would love her back. Robin frustratedly attempted to explain that even an aura as strong as hers would be an inadequate defense against a switchblade knife.

Secure, however, in her cosmic energy, the young woman ignored his warnings. One day Robin saw her stroll by a gang hanging out on a stoop. He crept a little closer, clenching his fists to defend her should the situation turn ugly. The guys carefully looked over this celestial vision floating down the street. A loud whistle pierced the air.

The young woman merely smiled and continued down the street. Robin slunk back to his apartment with his tail between his legs. He never brought up urban-warfare strategies again after being shown that sometimes the best defense is no defense at all.

During that second year at Juilliard, Robin also found that he was attractive to other women—large numbers of them. "I had one or two steady girlfriends in high school, but then in college, it was three, four . . . I went crazy. At one point I had three separate girlfriends, running around like mad."

Robin decided to spend his summer vacation recuperating back on the West Coast, and ended up falling head-over-heels in love with a California beauty.

After spending three dreamy months hiking in Marin, relaxing on the beach, taking in the sights of San Francisco, and enjoying each other, he had no urge to leave his lady and return to school in September. He was positive that this was no mere summer romance—it was the Real Thing. Juilliard paled by comparison.

The situation was exacerbated by the fact that his best buddy Christopher Reeve had also left school to act in a soap opera. There would be no one with whom he could commiserate. And school was even more difficult because third-year students no longer took formal classes. Instead, their training came from actual acting experiences: performing in road shows held in community centers out on Long Island or in the musty gyms of rowdy high schools up in the Bronx.

Loneliness was a deep pit lurking nearby, and Robin fell right into its trap again. He missed his California girl so badly that he began calling her every night, running up phone bills as high as $400 a month. His landlord was constantly threatening him about his overdue rent, and some nights he was so short on cash he had to skip dinner. The problems built up with an intense crescendo until Robin made his move. He went back to California to earn real money as an actor. And to be with his girlfriend.

Immediately upon arriving in California, Robin knew that he had made the right choice. He had been stagnating in New York. He needed to get out from under the safety net of his teachers and jump into untested professional waters on his own.

It was a joyous occasion when he was reunited with his love and they immediately got an apartment together. For a month everything was roses and candlelight, but little by little, the rapture began to fade. Robin had spent most of his savings on the flight back, and he found that the local theater companies weren't falling all over themselves to woo a Juilliard dropout into their fold. The rejections began to take their toll on him and he found it increasingly difficult to feel tremendously loving. As his situation slid from bad to ridiculous, Robin found himself dishing out frozen delights at an organic ice-cream parlor in Mill Valley to make ends meet.

It was also during this time that Robin first saw the devastating side of the drug culture. His girlfriend's casual experimentation was beginning to turn into addiction. Gradually, he saw her change from a sweet, gentle woman into a drug-crazed demon. Things finally got to the point where he couldn't stand seeing her that way any longer, and she was equally sick of his nagging. They went their separate ways.

Robin was miserable. And this time it was worse than in New York, because now he couldn't use being homesick as an excuse—he *was* home. Almost everyone he knew and loved was living within an hour's drive of his apartment.

Again he looked into the paying acting companies, and again nothing clicked. At that time in San Francisco, actors were faced with a catch-22 kind of situation: They had to actually be in a play to get into auditions but there weren't very many plays around to be in. So, desperate to work at anything even remotely connected to a stage, he checked out the local comedy scene.

"I couldn't get acting work, so I went to comedy workshops that were more or less improvisational theater," he said. "I got up once and did five or ten minutes of some old stuff and it went over pretty well. I thought, 'Wow, something's here.' "

One workshop, run by a man named Frank Kidder, performed on weekends in a coffeehouse called the Intersection, located in the basement of a Presbyterian church on Union Street. Warming up the audience before the comedy skits were avant-garde poets—many of them radical feminists—spouting incredibly off-the-wall free verse.

Robin quickly pulled together a standup routine and earned ten dollars his first night. "It was such a rush the first time I did it!" he exclaimed. "When I started performing standup comedy, I discovered this incredible new freedom, to go any place that occurred to me! From Shakespeare to rock 'n' roll, and I *loved* it!"

The audiences loved it, too. They laughed, they clapped, they thought he was great. Soon he found he could earn up to $25 a night—more than enough to cover his $100-a-month rent and still even eat frequently. Proudly self-sufficient, he could turn down his father's offers of cash.

Meanwhile, his dream of serious acting was temporarily put on ice, but Robin wasn't crying over spilled *Mikados*. "I decided I could either go mad or perform," he said about his depression after the breakup with his girlfriend. "I decided to go mad and perform at the same time. It wasn't bucks. It was the release I wanted."

Robin well remembered one of his first comedy gigs: warming up the crowd at his old alma mater, Marin Junior College, just before a heavy-metal concert. The audience consisted of thousands of heckling teenagers. One kid thought that throwing trash at the comic was a good game, and a frustrated Robin came extremely close to decking him with the microphone stand.

Gaining confidence and a following from the Intersection, Robin began branching out to other comedy clubs in the Bay Area. One club where he was a regular was the Salamander in Berkeley. This bar was so rough and tough that no one took any crap; Robin remembered one time when the manager shot a guy who asked for change.

An equally rough club he worked in frequently was called the Boarding House. The patrons would get so blitzed drinking beer that they would actually threaten the comedians with bodily injury if the jokes weren't funny. Once a guy even brought in a baseball bat and smacked it menacingly into his palm as he watched the show, daring the comedians to make him laugh.

Robin says that these threats helped him develop his unusual "duck-and-cover" style of breakneck patter. If something didn't work, wham! he went on to a completely different concept hoping that it would connect.

A member of the Bay Area comic clique from those days, Lorenzo Matawalan, met Robin in 1974 at the Intersection. He recalled the unassuming way Robin would get up on stage and do "a monster set," and then come back and ask his friends if he'd been okay. His pals called him

"Squirrel-Boy-Who-Turns-Into-Golden-Eagle-Onstage."

Matawalan said that Robin was the first local comedian to work at the Boarding House. Everyone in the clique considered it a "prestigious gig" and was grateful to Robin for opening the door. And Boarding House owner David Allen said that he was so taken with Robin's audition that "I immediately booked him."

The Holy City Zoo was another club where Robin occasionally performed, and was also the site of an extremely happy event. Robin liked hanging out in the tiny, smoky room so much that he would often help out behind the bar on nights when he didn't have a gig.

A cocktail waitress named Valerie Velardi—who was working at Zhivago's, a restaurant across the street—also liked catching a few laughs at the Holy City during her breaks. One night she noticed that the bartender was going through zillions of changes in his face every few minutes, and she became spellbound watching him. This character was so hilariously zany that she decided that she would rather watch him than the performers on the stage.

The feeling, it appeared, was mutual. "I saw this beautiful, crazy Italian woman and started trying to catch her attention by acting crazy," Robin remembered. "She wasn't dressed especially sexily; she just looked . . . hot. *Caliente*."

Robin jokingly told this woman that he was a French mime—speaking with an accent so authentic she fell for it. The next day he saw her again and tried out a Western drawl. When it dawned on her that perfect foreign accents were a major part of his act, she was laughing so hard that the deception didn't seem terrible at all.

Valerie began coming to the club more often, and before long she and Robin were a twosome. Robin can't even remember them having a first date—he thought that Valerie just came along to watch him perform somewhere. "A month after our first meeting we began to live together," Valerie said. "At that time I told him, 'You're the man who's going to marry me and give me my children.' "

She was right.

The daughter of a building contractor, Valerie grew up in New Haven, Connecticut. When she was twelve, her mother moved out after divorcing her father, and the responsibility of raising her three younger brothers and sister fell on Valerie's shoulders.

An all-encompassing love of dance brought her to San Francisco. She practiced for hours every day, even though she knew in her heart that she was already too old to consider performing as a professional career. When she met Robin she was twenty-six years old and was in the process of completing her masters degree in modern dance at Mill College near Oakland.

Valerie saw the promise, the spark of genius in the undisciplined Robin. His performances were brilliant, but his material was so scattered in his mental files that some of his best bits were never used or forgotten before he could work them into a routine. Realizing it was no cliché that Robin needed to get his act together, Valerie worked long hours with him to organize and catalogue his routines and jokes.

After that, things really began to take off. Robin began working at the best clubs in town, and his financial situation had improved tremendously. He and Valerie were even able to accompany some friends to Colorado for a Christmas skiing vacation.

For a while he was in a group called the Wing, which was like a division of the Committee. However, the Committee stuck to a regular routine and Robin's group performed total improvisation. One piece, called a "herald," could go on for an hour or two, depending on how into it the performers were, and was a completely freeform frolic through an insane psyche. The group, which included Joe Spano (later a star of the TV show *Hill Street Blues*), performed every Monday night and when the Committee was on tour.

During the summer of 1976, Robin and Valerie noticed that some San Francisco comics were beginning to break into big-time entertainment down in Los Angeles. A couple of locals had even gotten spots on *The Merv Griffin Show*. They both knew that if Robin wanted to get seriously into comedy, he would eventually end up in either Los Angeles or New York.

They talked long and hard about what they should do. Valerie had to remain in the Bay Area until she completed her degree, and Robin didn't really want to live away from her. He also felt bad that she would be giving up her own shot at a career, since Los Angeles wasn't exactly sending out frantic SOS signals for more modern-dance teachers.

After much soul searching, they decided that Robin should join the migration south, and Valerie would come down as soon as she could.

▪ 4 ▪

Dirty *Glasses,* Laughing at *Laugh-In,* and a *Pryor* Commitment

ONCE IN LOS ANGELES, ROBIN IMMEDIATELY GRAVItated towards Tinseltown's laugh clubs. He joined the long line of undiscovered comics one night at an open-mike tryout at the Comedy Store and was soon hired to perform for $200 a night on the main stage. Before long, Robin was working like mad all over town. "I was performing constantly—three times a night at different clubs—really cranking it out," he said.

All the TV and movie producers in town knew that the Comedy Store and another club, the Improvisation, were hotbeds of new talent. They often went there to find the perfect performer to fill a certain role. One such producer, George Schlatter, split his sides laughing at bearded, long-haired Robin's set of midnight-blue jokes. Schlatter told the young man to tone down his material, cut his hair, and shave—or he'd never get a job. Robin followed the suggestions, and Schlatter promptly hired him to perform in *The Great American Laugh-Off*.

Also around that time, Robin was one of the comedians signed during June of 1976 for a film called *Can I Do It . . . 'Til I Need Glasses?* Producers Mike Callie and Bob Levy owned several Laff Stop comedy stores, and filmed standup comics acting out raunchy routines.

Their first such film, *If You Don't Stop You'll Go Blind*, was released in 1975 and grossed between $15 and $20 million. The movie had no story; the producers simply filmed 150 actors and comics telling 172 dirty jokes over a period of 31 days, which was later cut down to 70 skits in approximately 80 minutes.

Glasses, which cost $750,000 to make, paid Robin $150 to act in two vignettes. In one he played the prosecuting attorney in an adultery case; in the other he was a man with a toothache who accidentally enters a gynecologist's office. Producer Callie described Robin's part as "G-rated material in an R-rated movie."

Although Robin was reportedly the most highly paid member of the 100-person cast (including 44 other standup comics) the movie ran a little too long, and his part was left out of the final version. (A show-biz insider said that Robin had been "desperate for that job. Like any struggling young actor, he would have taken almost any part that came his way at that point. He was working in all the comedy clubs, and knocking himself out trying to get a little recognition. I know he was terribly disappointed when his bit was cut out."

Robin's name didn't even get into an initial listing of the film's actors that ran in *Variety* in late July of 1976. Seventeen of the actors were listed in alphabetical order, but the list stopped at S.

Robin refused to get upset over this setback and worked even harder at his standup routine, hoping to attract further attention from the film community. It worked. George Schlatter had been so pleased with Robin's good nature and talent that he asked the comic to be a continuing performer on a TV program he was developing: the new *Laugh-In*.

After only six months in Los Angeles Robin was going to be a regular on a national TV show. He was ecstatic; he couldn't believe his luck. He called Valerie immediately with the good news and their happiness sent the phone wires between Los Angeles and San Francisco crackling. Since Robin's arrival in L.A. they had only seen each other on weekends, and the separation had been hard on both of them. But now Valerie had nearly completed her degree and she promised to hurry down for a celebration.

Robin was already making grandiose plans,

certain that this was his break into the big time. Soon he'd buy a mansion, a limo, hire servants. . . .

Rowan and Martin's Laugh-In, produced by George Schlatter from 1968 to 1973, was undeniably one of TV's most innovative, fast-paced, and funny shows. Unknowns like Goldie Hawn, Lily Tomlin, Jo-Anne Worley, Judy Carne, Gary Owens, and Ruth Buzzi gained overnight superstardom for their zany characterizations. Who could ever forget the German soldier (Arte Johnson) who lurked behind bushes and thought everything was "verrry interesting," or the little old lady who would wallop the dirty old man offering Walnettos with her purse?

"Sock it to me!" "Here come de judge," and "Beautiful downtown Burbank" became national slogans. ("The Fickle Finger of Fate" even made it into the lyrics of a hit song by the Supremes.) The insane jokes came unrelentingly fast and furious for the show's entire hour—from actors popping out of the joke wall or on the undulating body of a woman in a bikini—and the country went crazy for the show's clever hipness. It was the number-one program its first two seasons on the air.

Talk about your proverbial hard act to follow.

Robin went to the first rehearsal for the new *Laugh-In* thinking it would be a breeze, but the cold hard reality of the show's failure was like a tray of ice cubes dumped down his back. He once likened the experience to making *Jaws VI*—how can you surpass such a landmark original?

The revival, which aired on NBC as a series of six specials during the 1977–1978 season, failed to capture both the lighthearted freshness of the original as well as a large audience. Robin found himself generally playing two scarlet-hued characters: a Russian and a red-neck.

He remembered one time being afraid that his best line would get him canned from the show. He had gone up to guest star Frank Sinatra and said: "Mr. Sinatra, I'm so happy to meet you I could drop a log." Fortunately, the singer liked the joke so it didn't become an issue.

Robin's lucky streak held, even though *Laugh-In*'s didn't. Before the show bit the dust, he was hired as a featured performer on *The Richard Pryor Show.* Unfortunately, it was another ill-fated program, lasting only from September 13, 1977 until October 20, 1977—a grand total of five shows.

Pryor was definitely the rising black comedian when the show began, and NBC had hoped to cash in on the popularity he had gained through his nightclub act, appearances on talk shows, and burgeoning movie career. His original contract had been for a minimum of ten shows, but thanks to a combination of the success from his movies *Silver Streak* and *Greased*

Lightning and problems with the censors, both NBC and Pryor agreed to cut that number in half.

Although Pryor went into the show with high hopes, his battle with the censors was the stuff legends are made of. Used to total freedom in his nightclub act, he could use any subject as the foil of his outrageous wit and satire. But TV clamped on the shackles from the opening shot of his first show. In that scene, the comedian was shown nude from the waist up, commenting on how he hadn't lost anything while bickering with the censors. Then the camera panned down and showed his entire torso, which was both totally nude and devoid of any sexual organs (he had been wearing a body stocking). Photos of the scene appeared on every newscast shown that day and in newspapers, including *The New York Times*, but the segment was completely cut from the show because it was deemed obscene.

Near the end of the run, Pryor was so frustrated by all of television's do's and don't's that he began acting out his old nightclub routines verbatim in front of the camera. From the forty to forty-five minutes of monologue recorded, only three or four minutes ever appeared on the air.

Despite these problems, Robin did have a lot of fun performing on the show because the comics were actually given quite a bit of freedom.

After the show ended, Robin found himself at loose ends again. He got another little nibble of work—playing Jason Shine, the laidback surfer-gigolo on the comedy talk show *America 2Nite*—but Robin really wanted a bigger chunk of steady work.

Around this time he was in an improvisation workshop run by Harvey Lembeck (remembered for the roles of Eric Von Zipper in *Beach Blanket Bingo* and Harry Shapiro in *Stalag 17*). One night the audience included Larry Brezner, an associate agent with the firm Joffe, Rollins, Morra & Brezner, whose clients included comics such as Woody Allen, Robert Klein, and Martin Mull.

Lembeck would call out situations and have the students make up some sort of a routine around them. Brezner sat in stunned silence watching Robin work. No matter what kind of a crazy or improbable idea was tossed out, Robin would never lose his place.

"I watched two hours of this kid never losing, reacting off the top of his head, working off nerve impulses—not intellect at all," Brezner remembered. "Incredible. He wasn't much different onstage then; the attitudes were all the same. He's like Holden Caulfield, a guy walking around with all his nerve endings completely exposed."

He immediately signed Robin into his fold.

Another member of Lembeck's group was John

Ritter (who then made his way to fame on TV's *Three's Company*). He vividly recalled how Robin was dressed—the baggy pants and suspenders, or a shabby tuxedo with high-topped basketball shoes and a raggedy straw hat—and figured that Robin was merely interested in getting sight gags. "So I watched carefully, and he turned out to be the funniest guy I've ever seen."

A short time later producer Garry Marshall took his nine-year-old son, Scotty, to see the movie *Star Wars*. Like almost everyone else in the country at that time, Scotty was enraptured by the film. He begged his dad to put an extraterrestrial on "their" show—*Happy Days*. The elder Marshall noticed that outer-space fever was sweeping the country and decided that this wasn't such a bad idea.

A script was worked up where an alien named Mork would land in Milwaukee and decide to take Fonzie back to his planet as a souvenir. Dom De Luise was first offered the part, but his manager wouldn't let him work on series television. The next actor asked was Jonathan Winters, but he was just about to leave for a tour of Australia.

John Byner was finally cast as Mork, but at 11:00 A.M. on the day rehearsals were to begin, he changed his mind and begged off the role, saying, "I can't do this. He's not a real person." The producers were forced to close down the set while they looked for a new alien. They immediately called all the agents in town, announcing an open audition.

The show's producer-director, Jerry Paris (of *The Dick Van Dyke Show* fame), said that the fifty actors who tried out began arriving about one o'clock. "They were all terrible. About five o'clock in walked this boy with rainbow suspenders. When he sat down I asked him if he could sit a little differently, the way an alien might. Immediately he sat on his head. We hired him and when the show was over, he gave me the suspenders."

During the audition Robin said the producers gave him almost no direction, so he made every bizarre sound, voice, and movement he could dream up.

The "Mork" episode of *Happy Days* aired in February of 1978. Robin's performance was brilliant, and he even upstaged Henry Winkler, who played the Fonz, that year's popular character on TV. The avalanche of fan mail that flooded into the studio was the largest in the history of the four-year-old show. ABC quickly asked Marshall to develop a spin-off, and *Mork and Mindy* was born without even making a pilot show.

"Just think of it," Robin mused, "a nine-year-old kid was responsible for my career."

▪ 5 ▪

Mork Blasts Off

NO ONE WAS READY FOR THE SUCCESS OF *MORK AND Mindy*. Not the producers, not the critics, not even the stars. In fact, most people in Hollywood were gleefully rubbing their hands together and waiting for the show to quickly wither up and crawl off to that dusty graveyard where obscure TV programs are buried.

"When *Mork and Mindy* premiered, the critics were just waiting for the show to bomb," said Bruce Johnson, supervising producer and one of the show's writers. "They couldn't imagine doing a show about someone from outer space.

"It was like a flashback to the sixties, with shows like *My Favorite Martian* and *Bewitched*. All those people who predicted the show would fail had not yet met or heard of Robin Williams.

"Looking back on *Mork and Mindy*'s premise, it's obvious why everyone thought it would be such a disaster—a new show in 1978 about an alien named Mork from a planet called Ork who comes to earth in an egg and lives with a girl named Mindy in Boulder, Colorado. It sure sounds like Saturday morning fare to me. I don't know whether I'd have watched it.

"The fact that the show came from the Garry Marshall camp didn't help either. The critics weren't fans of Garry's shows, although millions of viewers adored them."

The only indication that the show might have been something special came during the taping of the first program. "Most of the time, the studio audience for a new show is down," said the show's director Howard Storm. "They don't know the characters. With *Mork,* they went crazy."

That spring and summer before the show was aired was a wonderful time for Robin and Valerie. They were in love and on top of the world. Robin would be earning $15,000 per episode, for twenty-six weeks! The previous year he thought he had done pretty well with his nightclub act, sometimes earning $700 a night. "But it wasn't a great year financially," he said. He earned about $20,000 during 1977.

Although it was staggering to think that he would be earning nearly as much in a week as he used to make in a year, Robin and Valerie refused to get caught up in a big money trip, stoutly insisting that they weren't interested in buying lavish material things. For the time being they decided to continue living in the small, one-bedroom Hollywood apartment Robin had rented when he first came to Los Angeles. And since show business's unpredictability is such a large part of the beast, they decided not to count their millions while the checks were still in the mail.

The one thing they decided they were ready for was a greater commitment to each other. On June 4, 1978, Robin and Valerie were married on the top of a hill overlooking San Francisco Bay, surrounded by his family (they planned a second reception in New Haven during the fall for Valerie's family) and all their friends.

A comedian friend from L.A. remembered the joyous occasion as "a simply beautiful day. Robin looked dashing and was smiling the whole time. Valerie was absolutely gorgeous. After this romantic outdoor wedding we all went for a marvelous dinner with loads of champagne. There were comedians and mimes performing all evening long. It was a fantastic party."

Afterwards, Robin and Valerie flew to a romantic island where there was absolutely nothing to do. Still, she nearly had to tie him to palm trees to make him slow down and relax a little. "Our honeymoon was the only time I didn't perform," he said, "and then I was looking for microphones and making them out of coconuts."

Settling into the three-room apartment, the couple immediately began filling it with exotic pets: a parrot named Cora who was fond of screeching out "parrots can't talk" and nibbling on sliced green grapes, a lizard named Truman Capote (because he had no neck), and an iguana named Mister E.

While Valerie got jobs teaching modern dance at two local colleges, Robin began spending all his daylight hours at Paramount Studios filming *Mork and Mindy*. Because his previous TV acting experience was so limited, Robin would have probably known just as much about it if he had really just arrived from Ork in a big flying egg. But he caught on fast and soon had everyone in the cast doubled over with laughter at his wit.

Being a relative novice may have actually helped Robin in his role as Mork—he didn't realize that acting on the show was supposed to be hard work. He had so much fun that all the cast and crew members were caught up in his infectious joy.

"It was a simply magical time," Johnson said. "Every taping was full of wonderful surprises. It was like a happening. On most shows there's someone you don't like, but everyone involved with *Mork and Mindy* was great. We had cast parties every Friday night at a terrible restaurant around the corner from the studio. Robin would come up into the audience between scenes and perform pieces of his nightclub routine or improvise something. Sometimes the show had to work hard to keep up with the between-the-scenes antics.

"All of it was due to Robin's sheer genius and creativity. I've produced twenty shows, but I've never worked with such an extraordinary raw talent as his. He truly made the show—no other actor could have given Mork the sensitivity and subtle nuances that made him a completely believable character."

The producers recognized Robin's talent and often gave him free rein, allowing him to improvise routines and lines at will. They did not, however, merely leave whole parts of the script open except for the notation "Robin does his thing," as was frequently reported when the show was new.

"There's no way we could have left blank parts in the script," Johnson explained. "It was a three-camera show, meaning each scene is blocked down to the Nth degree because two of the cameras are responsible for doing closeups. If an actor isn't right on his mark during the filming, it throws off the preplanned distance and the shot is out of focus.

"Every word of the show was scripted, but we did let Robin make up lines and *schtick* whenever he wanted. The only problem was keeping his interest up between the first rehearsal on Monday and the final taping on Friday. He'd think up a hilarious piece of business on Tuesday, then get bored with it by Thursday and want to put in something else. We had the darndest time getting him to leave it alone. He'd say, 'That's old already,' and we'd say, 'But Robin, the *audience* hasn't seen it yet!' He was so fast, so clever, he always wanted to be off on something new."

Johnson said that when something didn't work, Robin was the first one to throw it out. "Sometimes he'd come up with a new gag on a Friday that he'd fall in love with, and spring it on the audience. If it didn't work, he'd apologize for blowing the line, then ask to redo the scene, and would do the lines the way they were written. He had absolutely no ego."

Used to working at his own pace doing improvisation anyway, Robin was completely comfortable with the show's loose format. He warmed up to the fact that his kinky brand of humor was appreciated, and would pull zany pranks on the cast and crew.

His frequent foil was costar Pam Dawber, who didn't meet Robin until they were both cast for the show. Robin was having his makeup done for a test shooting when Pam walked in with a big smile on her face and introduced herself as Mindy. Robin spoke to her for about two minutes in a mix of something that sounded like Russian and terribly broken English, a variation of the gag he had pulled on Valerie the first time they met. Pam fell for it hook, line, and sinker. Walking out of the room, she wondered how in the world they were going to do the show around that horrible accent of his.

"Robin was always doing something to break Pam up," Johnson said. "A couple of times she would be yelling for him to come down from his room in the attic because he'd done something bad, only to glance up and see him standing there—out of sight of the audience—totally nude. She really freaked out the first couple of times. Another time he was wearing a towel, but dropped it to the floor and mooned the audience as he left the stage. One time she asked him to bring something down from his room, and he showed up with an inflatable woman.

"Some of the funniest—and most unprintable—things he did were after Mork and Mindy got married and would be in bed together. He would have a gas attack and time it just before her lines, so she couldn't breathe. Or he'd have crazy fights with her under the covers or bring certain unmentionable props into bed. Sure it was tacky, but it was so funny."

But Pam loved Robin as much as Mindy loved Mork. He could do no wrong in her eyes, even though she always saw clearly through all his silly tricks. "Robin's purity of spirit is so unmistakable, so winning," she said. "There's nobody who doesn't want to hurt others as much as Robin doesn't. There's no anger in him."

They would often socialize off the set as well, going out to dinner or roller skating together with Valerie and/or Pam's current flame. When Robin was too busy she would "miss him terribly" and said that working together so closely was similar to being married.

Robin also taught Pam a tremendous amount of "acting street smarts." She'd been in a couple of plays before, but was also a novice to work on television. "Robin respected her so much," Johnson said. "He always stood stock still when Pam said her lines; he never tried to upstage her or step on her lines. There was no need."

Robin's wild interpretation of Mork made the show a refreshing change of pace from the usual staid sitcoms, while his imaginative repartee brought in a much broader-based audience than the producers expected.

"We really designed the show to be successful on two levels," Johnson explained. "There was stuff for the kids on one level. They wouldn't understand the stuff on the other level but they didn't miss anything that was going on because they could see his antics. He would physicalize so well he would cover the intellectualisms and philosophies. Yes, it was a silly show and yes, it was for children, but it also sent adults running for their dictionaries."

Some of Robin's best sight gags naturally had a limited life. After all, how many times can you laugh at a person sitting on his head or sucking up water through his index finger (even though it does allow him to simultaneously drink and speak without drooling)? Sensing that, Robin stuck to what he does best—rapid fire one-liners and off-the-universe comments. Some of his throwaway lines were funnier than entire seasons of other series.

"He had nuances in his performance that a normal actor wouldn't even conceive of," Johnson said. "No one else would even think to try to go to the places where Robin went. He was, and is, totally fearless and will do anything."

Nothing seemed too ridiculous or too dumb to try. There was the memorable time Robin fell in love with a department store mannequin, or the way he would seriously discuss things with stuffed moose heads and plants, unwilling to risk offending anyone (or anything) he came across on this strange planet. He wanted to liberate all the people trapped in the refrigerator tray's eggs (since Orkans are born in eggs), wore his watch on his ankle, ate plastic, and got drunk on cream soda.

Consider Robin's coining of the Orkan language: Parents across the country were immediately subjected to massive doses of "nanu-nanu" and "shazbot" ad infinitum.

"You've got to be crazy," Robin asserted. "You're only given a little spark of madness, and it must be preserved at any cost."

Others were paid to see that that "spark of madness" didn't flare up into a wildfire of lunacy. "Everybody here is aware that this is really *The Robin Williams Show*," said director Howard Storm. "My job is to make sure Robin doesn't go so far off-the-wall that only seven people in the audience understand what he's doing."

Storm added that the other characters were cast with people who could hold their own against Robin's improvisation. Tom Poston as the grouchy landlord Mr. Bickley was a perfect foil for Mork's innocent sweetness, while Robert Donner's Exidor was so crazy that he actually made Mork seem seminormal. Conrad Janis played Mindy's conservative dad with a cool, unflappable manner, and Elizabeth Kerr was very funny as Mindy's free-spirited grandmother.

The combination was an immediate, unbelievable success. Even though everyone in the cast was superb, all the wagging fingers of responsibility were pointed straight at Robin. Robert MacKenzie of *TV Guide* wrote: "If Williams's wild talents were at all repressible, the series would sink like an iron duck."

A pre-airing review printed in the *Los Angeles Times* on the show's debut night, September 14, 1978, said that the reader "may be excused for thinking that *The Clone Master*, as bad as it is, has got to be better than what is suggested by the premise of the new comedy series *Mork and Mindy*," which sounded suspiciously like "outdated, gimmicky series such as *Bewitched* or *I Dream of Jeannie*." But a paragraph later it conceded that "*Mork and Mindy* is a prime contender for the best new comedy of the season."

Richard Hack of the *Hollywood Reporter* wrote that the show "is one of those series which suffers at the hand of its own description . . . taken at face value it should be a mixture of silly one-liners mixed with a healthy scoop of physical slapstick. Lucky for us all that *nothing* seems to have been taken at face value here." He concluded that it was a "sure pick hit—period."

"I had a couple of guys I know working at major newspapers call me up saying they have never been so misinformed and wrong in their lives," Johnson remembered about the show's debut.

Once the media picked up on the show, Robin skyrocketed to fame. Almost overnight he went from a nobody who could go anyplace and do anything he pleased to a virtual prisoner of his own success.

Robin was the person most surprised by the

rapid rise of the show. "It's amazing, I can't believe it," he said at the time. "I wasn't confident about *Mork and Mindy* succeeding when we went on the air. I knew the show was good, but I also knew a lot of good shows die because of their time slots. We were up against *The Waltons* and that's pretty powerful competition."

Mork and Mindy was constantly in the top ten of the Nielsen ratings during its first year. In February of 1979, it hit number one and by March was averaging a viewing audience of 53 million people every week. It was the number three show during the 1978–79 season.

The amazing popularity of the show that first year made it impossible to get tickets to the filming or rehearsals. Even though the tickets to TV tapings are free, Johnson said that people were getting caught outside the studio for scalping tickets for five or ten dollars.

"We tried to warn Robin what was ahead, but I think the idea was inconceivable to him for a while," Johnson said. "I walked him out to his car the night after the *Time* magazine with his face on the cover hit the stands. This was literally two or three weeks after the show first aired. At the time he didn't think he'd really become so famous.

"A few nights later Dale McRaven, Garry Marshall, and I had a meeting with him and Pam about what the press situation was going to be.

We explained that they would get beaten up and adulation all at the same time.

"This was just before we went to a party at the Century Plaza Hotel where all three networks entertain the TV writers from around the country. The place went crazy when he walked in. Even though we had tried to brief Robin and Pam on what to expect, I could tell they both were blown away at the end of the night. It's a shocking experience—there's no real way to prepare someone for something like that.

"At the time Robin said to me, 'I don't know how to handle this. Every way I turn someone wants something from me.' Intellectually he was on top of it. He knew what he should and shouldn't do. But basically he's a very honest person so it's very difficult for him to edit himself when he is speaking. What he thinks, he says."

In addition to being honest, Robin tends to be on the shy side when he's not in front of the camera or on stage. He has explained that this shyness affects his speaking voice: He sounds a little Scottish, because of a tendency to drop off the ends of words.* Visitors to the *Mork and*

---

*At the beginning of the media madness Robin was so intimidated by giving interviews that he actually led interviewers to believe he was Scottish. Several early interviews—including one by Cecil Smith in the *Los Angeles Times*—mention that he was born in Scotland.

Mindy set were often amazed that this wildman of comedy could be sitting so sedately in a corner observing what was going on.

When the show first started filming, the costumers asked Robin what he wanted to wear. He suggested his own wardrobe, explaining that since no one knows what is worn by the dapper follower of fashion in space, he might as well be comfortable. His wardrobe included his own baggy pants purchased at Aardvark's Odd Ark (a used-clothing store in West Hollywood) held up by rainbow suspenders with various badges and buttons dangling off at rakish angles, all topped off with wild Hawaiian shirts or crazy-colored tee shirts.

His conspicuous dress immediately made him a marked Mork. Kids would rush up to him on the street, screaming, "Mork, Mork!" and beg him to take them up in space with him. One day he was enjoying his usual afternoon skate in his favorite part of town, the free-for-all carnival along the Venice boardwalk. Robin cruised into a pay phone to make a call and suddenly found himself surrounded on all sides by fans who nearly tipped the booth over in their eagerness to see their hero in the flesh. "I felt like I was in the San Diego Zoo," he said. After that the only skating he did in Venice was extremely fast speed-skating. Otherwise, he'd glide around the Paramount lot during his lunch hour.

"His popularity did grow to be a problem, but no more than for someone like Larry Hagman [who plays J.R. Ewing on the TV soap, *Dallas*]," Johnson said. "It may have been different since Robin was popular with young people, who are louder. When we traveled around the country we would get mobbed the same as a rock star. It disrupted his lifestyle in that he would have to go to friends' homes with private beaches to hang out. He couldn't just go out in public like he used to."

Robin began keeping a box of sand in his dressing room to wiggle his toes in whenever he got lonely for the beach.

Johnson added that "the most hairy point" he could remember was a show they filmed at Mile High Stadium during a football game between the Denver Broncos and the Kansas City Chiefs. In that segment Mork joined the Broncos cheerleaders. "We had to surround him with a wedge of twenty police to get him from place to place."

After all the craziness broke loose, Robin and Valerie rented a two-room apartment on Zuma beach to use as a retreat. "I need this little place on the beach for sanity. I don't like to tell people where we live because we treasure privacy. We have an iguana that will eat anybody who comes near our place in town!" he warned at the time.

In addition to the beach house, Robin's only real extravagance that first fall was taking out a lease on a 1976 Volvo. He and Valerie had three other cars, two of which were junkers that they left wherever they happened to break down. Robin has joked that it was like being a part of the pony express. Later on he bought a used Land Rover.

For a time Robin had a used Austin-Healey he loved to death. One day it was stolen while parked right in front of his apartment building. He asked his landlord how such a thing could happen in broad daylight without anyone seeing it, and the landlord told Robin that he had seen a group of young men pushing the car down the street. When the shocked actor asked why the incident hadn't been reported immediately to the police, the landlord replied that he had assumed the men were a group of Robin's comedian friends who were merely borrowing the vehicle.

Once *Mork*'s success took off, it immediately led to the usual myriad of licensed products. There were Mork posters, Mork tee shirts, Mork dolls—even Mork gum that came in little eggs. (Robin didn't want the gum on the market because it contained sugar, but it was released despite his protests.)

Robin proudly told people that he was carefully placing this influx of income in such solid investments as "land in Nicaragua and the Jerusalem oil fields," while Valerie really tucked away the cash in the bank.

Despite all the money flowing in, Robin's favorite pastime was still performing in front of an audience, which he usually did for no pay. After a full day working on *Mork and Mindy* he'd zoom off to the Comedy Store or Off-the-Wall, where he'd sneak in the back door and surprise the late-late crowd with a stunning performance.

"Performing for me is an incomparable high. A drug," he has been fond of saying. "Finding something new onstage, a new comic plateau, is . . . so Zenlike. Because the essence of comedy is indescribable. Try to define it, and it falls apart; but when it works, there is no higher place."

"He gets so excited about performing that I have to drag him back home," said Valerie.

When she finally did get him home, Robin liked to stay there. They rarely went out to dinner, enjoying instead the delicious vegetarian meals Valerie would whip up while her husband listened to everything from Bach to the Beach Boys. He would frequently tease the woman he affectionately called Pooky, Miss V, or Venus about her pastaless pasta dishes crammed with zucchini, tomato sauce, and a mystery vegetable he named "Velardi squash."

In an effort to keep Robin's image on a slightly higher level than a normal TV superstar, his managers refused to let him do commercials. Robin never forgot Mr. Rollins's first assessment of him: "The talent is endless; the discipline is nil."

Valerie begged to differ, saying that Robin was not undisciplined, he was "simply lazy, although he has inexhaustible energy for the things he considers fun, like roller skating and getting attention from pretty girls."

In December of 1978, Robin and Valerie felt comfortable enough with Robin's success to purchase a $200,000 house situated on a huge lot in Topanga Canyon, close to the beach. Immediately, they began adding exotic pets to their menagerie: chickens incapable of laying eggs, a Malamute named Sam, and two dwarf goats named Carlos and Carlotta.

They both adored the place, its wildness, and the way it reminded them of what they still considered to be "home"—northern California. Because the Topanga house was at least an hour's drive from Hollywood, they kept their "seedy" apartment so Robin would have a place to stay during late nights. The problem was that he began having more and more late nights, and seeing Valerie less and less.

▪ 6 ▪

"I Yam What I Yam"

JUST TWO MONTHS AFTER *MORK AND MINDY* BURST into living rooms across America, Robin's fame was such that he was flooded with offers for work. Companies wanted him to do commercials endorsing their products. Producers were sending in piles of film offers.

Attempting to protect their young client's interests, Robin's managers told everyone that his acting talents would be reserved for *Mork* and a maximum of one movie a year.

Together with friend Bennett Tramer, Robin was busily working on a screenplay he likened to an "early, early Woody Allen movie." Realizing this wouldn't be complete for quite some time, he examined the scripts he had received and picked one that Dustin Hoffman had originally agreed to do with Lily Tomlin.

After reading the script, Hoffman had told

director Robert Altman that he thought it was ill-conceived and recommended that screenwriter Jules Feiffer be given the heave-ho. Altman dumped Hoffman instead, a first in movie-industry history, and decided that having the hottest alien on earth as his star wouldn't hurt his flick.

On March 27, 1979, Robin signed to play the lead role in Robert Altman's movie *Popeye,* a role he said "was like being asked to play Buddha."

Feiffer said the role of Popeye would have been "a reach for Hoffman. The character has a warmth under all his violence. Robin Williams is perfect."

Lily Tomlin backed out of the deal after Robin was signed, and Gilda Radner was next courted for Olive's role. Feiffer nixed her as second choice because he thought that two comics playing these cartoon characters opposite each other might be a bit much.

Right away, the Paramount publicity mill began cranking out the tons of press that would inundate the American public for the next year. Included was an ad on *Saturday Night Live* announcing: "Robin Williams in his first screen role. Star of *Mork and Mindy* in the funniest, most outrageous comedy hit of the year."

Wrong. Robin's first role on the big screen had ended up on a cutting room floor. No fools they—upon noticing Robin's astonishing success, Mike Callie and Bob Levy immediately began searching for the previously discarded footage Robin acted in for *Can I Do It . . . 'Til I Need Glasses.*

After two weeks of viewing 125,000 feet of film hidden away in mislabeled canisters, the pair came upon the clips. "Suddenly, we knew exactly how John Sutter [the man who first discovered gold in California] felt," Callie said, remembering that they "got very paranoid for no reason" and immediately locked up the film in a safety deposit box. The following Monday he and Levy halted distribution on the film, had all eighty prints returned to them, and added Robin's three-and-one-half minutes of skits. When the film was re-released, the ads shouted about Robin's *real* first film role and gave him top billing.

"It's no more deceptive than billing Marlon Brando as the star of *Superman* for a four-minute performance or billing him as the star of *Apocalypse Now* for a ten-minute appearance," Callie said.

Robin and his management team felt a bit differently. Calling the advertising "false and misleading," they quickly filed legal action to get the ads modified. They also demanded $5 million in punitive damages.

But even court orders and bad reviews couldn't

stop the hordes of people who began flooding into theaters to view their favorite rave. The *Los Angeles Times* called the film "a randy and obsolete movie which got some mileage out of the Robin Williams lawsuit." *Variety* said the movie was "a juvenile, unfunny screen version of some of the oldest and worst sex jokes in comedy history," adding that it probably never would have resurfaced "but because popular vidstar Robin Williams has a minuscule role (not even contained in the original version), the film finds itself back at theaters boasting the screen debut of the TV actor."

Callie said the film grossed about $3 million and added: "Robin was the key we needed to get playdates. Some audiences may be unhappy that Robin's appearance is so brief, but then they discover that the rest of the film is very funny. This isn't a ripoff. The movie's been held over in lots of situations."

He insisted that he didn't want credit for discovering Robin . . . "but I did help him along. I kept him working for a year and a half. His management now says that I'm hurting his image." Besides, Callie added, none of Robin's scenes were as blue as the jokes on the comedian's own album.

The suit finally came before the court in late February of 1981. Robin made a five-minute appearance in Los Angeles Superior Court, which ended with both parties agreeing to a modification in the film's advertising campaign.

Before strapping on the massive latex forearms that would help transform him into Popeye, Robin flexed his comic muscles a couple of different ways. First he demanded that ABC double his salary to $30,000 per episode and give him a larger share of *Mork and Mindy*'s profits before he would renew his contract. The producers could hardly refuse—no Robin, no Mork. No Mork, no series.

And Robin's salary from *Popeye*, $500,000 plus points, was quite a step up from what he had earned in his first film role. But money was really meaningless to him, confided manager Charles Joffe. "When I made the *Popeye* deal with Paramount, Robin didn't ask me the terms for three months. He just didn't care. I don't think he knows how we handled the renegotiations on his television contract. That doesn't interest him. What interests him is his work."

In fact, even though he was earning megabucks, he still traveled around with only a few dollars in his pocket. Once when visiting New York and about to take a cab across town with a comedienne pal who hadn't yet hit the big time, Robin suggested that they split the cab fare. A third friend, overhearing the conversation, pulled Robin aside and quietly told him that considering his financial circumstances, he should really pick up the tab. Robin blushed, immediately apologized profusely to the woman, then asked his pal to loan him twenty bucks.

That fall Robin signed with Casablanca Records to make a live comedy album, called "Reality, What A Concept." Recorded during performances at the Boarding House in San Francisco and the Copacabana in New York, the audiences were obviously infatuated with Robin's every move—which made it a little frustrating for the listener who couldn't actually *see* what the heck happened on stage. The audiences were also a little too vocal in requesting Mork, which Robin adamantly refused to get caught up doing in concert. Nevertheless, Robin created a fantastic album, one which pleased both the public and the press. It quickly went platinum.

Lawrence Christon of the *Los Angeles Times* wrote that the album had "a couple of clunker jokes," then went on to say that it "gives summary evidence of why Williams is the hottest comic going." Christon commented favorably on the way Robin can "create and enact whole scenarios" in a multitude of different accents, and despite the numerous drug references, "most of the material is original and inspired."

Writing for *Us* magazine, Martha Hume noted the same problems inherent in a comedy album, then said: "Once the comic hits his stride, however, he puts in a great performance." She was also very impressed with Robin's range of characters, adding: "It becomes obvious that a guy this talented probably does Mork while his brain is at the dry cleaners."

The album was nominated for two Grammys and won the award for Best Comedy Album of the year.

After getting his huge raise, Robin breezed into his second year on *Mork and Mindy.* The show's first year had been a smashing triumph—the press was oozing with compliments, the public counted the hours between one show's final "Nanu-nanu" and the next week's egg landing, the cast had the best time of their lives, and even ABC executives were beside themselves with their megahit.

In all their glorious wisdom, however, during the show's second year ABC executives did the unthinkable. They committed the cardinal sin in TV programming: They messed with a hit.

First, Mindy's dad and grandmother were booted out and three new younger characters were trotted on. Jay Thomas and Gina Hecht costarred as brother and sister Remo and Jean DaVinci, who ran the New York Deli; Jim Staahl was cast in the part of Mindy's aggressive cousin, Nelson Flavor; Tom Poston's role was also cut back to an occasional guest appearance.

Then, stories were altered. Cutesy fables of an innocent learning about all the odd foibles of earthlings were no longer meaty enough. Relevant and serious subjects like the effect of advertising on consumers, life and death, love and friendship, were discussed. Some of these "meaningful" stories had bizarre settings or story twists where Mork would shrink and enter another world, or some such visual gimmick.

Next, *Mork* was whisked out of its nice cozy Thursday night time slot and plunked down on Sunday, opposite *Archie Bunker's Place*. Because *Mork* was the hottest show to come around since *All in the Family*, ABC was hoping that their fresh-faced alien would knock the socks off the tired old bigot. Unfortunately, the new stories flopped and the bigot still had some life in him. By midseason, the show had lost half its viewing audience and dropped to number forty.

In the midst of all this upheaval, Robin was spending every second he could training for his role in *Popeye*. During lunch breaks and after rehearsals, he would rush into the Paramount gym and practice tap dancing, handstands, and mulekicks for two hours a day with acrobatic dancer Lou Wills. The high level of activity helped Robin shed fifteen pounds to achieve the sinewy look of the cartoon character.

Preparation for the role began nine months before Robin appeared in front of a camera. He watched nearly fifty hours of original cartoons produced by Fleischer Studios during the thirties and forties and poured through thousands of comic strips to get into Popeye's character. He also took singing lessons so he could hold up his end of the tunes.

Right after Christmas in 1979, Robin and Valerie took off for Malta, which Robin described as "San Quentin on Valium." The rocky Mediterranean island, south of Sicily and north of Libya, is inhabited by an unvanquished race with a propensity for speaking both English and their Arabic-sounding tongue at the top of their voices. The crew was enclosed in a barbed-wire compound with guards at the front gates to keep the locals out.

Inside these wires was a $1,200,000 vision of Sweethaven, the New England fishing town Popeye drifts into after being lost at sea. Sweethaven had everything a town needed to survive—stingy greengrocer, café, saloon, barber shop, rooming house, and even a nearby house of ill "repuke," all slightly off-kilter and rakishly askew.

Popeye was a project that started off sounding too good to be true and ended up being not quite good enough. The wealth of talent working on the film was simply staggering: In addition to hit producer Robert Evans (*The Odd Couple, The Godfather, Love Story*), controversial but talented director Robert Altman (*Nashville, M*A*S*H*), satirist-cartoonist-playwright Jules

Feiffer penning the script, and songs by Harry Nilsson, the costars included Shelley Duvall as Olive Oyl and former Martian Ray Walston as Popeye's Pappy. Sweet Pea was played by Wesley Ivan Hurt, Altman's adorable five-month-old grandson, who stole the show with his darling expressions and grew so much during the six months on the island that he had to be wrapped in progressively larger swaddling clothes. Valerie was also working on the set warming up the dancers, and even had a small dancing part listed at the bottom of the screen credits.

When the cast and crew arrived on the barren beachfront that would be their home for the next six months, the half-year-long rainy season immediately began. Shooting around the clouds slowly began to dampen everyone's high spirits, partly because there was absolutely nothing entertaining to do during the long off-hours. There were a couple of pubs where the crew would hang out, drinking a ghastly concoction of chemicals the locals called wine and swapping lies from past lives back in civilization. Paul Dooley, who played the role of Wimpy, described the social scene under the occasionally burning Mediterranean sun: "When you're bored you can go to a rock concert. On Malta, that's eight people sitting around in a circle staring at a rock."

Getting ready for their roles took the better part of the morning for Robin and Shelley Duvall.

Shelley had to wear a three-piece wig that was held in place with ninety-three hairpins, plus outrageously enormous shoes that made her feet ache. After nearly an hour of being made-up, Robin had the huge latex forearms strapped on so tightly that his own arms often froze up in the middle of a fight scene from the lack of circulation, and he would be forced to stop the shooting and have them loosened up to get his blood flowing again.

Along with all the acrobatics involved in his role, Robin needed to keep one eye perpetually screwed up, as well as speak in what he described as a "liquid wrench" voice out of one corner of his mouth while simultaneously clenching a corncob pipe between his teeth. Robin achieved Popeye's gravel-like voice by pushing his voice down two levels, and using the deeper of the two for the sailor's ruminating mumbles.

Popeye's history also intimidated Robin. "Everyone [in the world] knows him," he said. "That's scary. It's more scary than doing Hamlet, because you can do Hamlet knowing [audiences] accept variations. People have seen Popeye change slightly but with the same big arms, one eye, and pipe for fifty years."

During his first conversation about the role with the producer, "Evans looked at me and said, 'You are him, I am him, you are what you are . . .' And I walked out of his office going,

'Yes, I can. Yes, I am. I am. I am. Sure I can.' I felt like the little actor that could." Robin knew that he had to be faithful to the well-loved Popeye while still injecting his own humanity into the character.

Playing Olive Oyl was equally challenging for Shelley Duvall, especially coming right on the heels of her role in *The Shining* where she did little but be chased by Jack Nicholson. Calling the role a "real treat," Duvall added that Olive was the first "woman of any strength" she was able to play. "Olive Oyl is one-hundred-and-one percent woman. She's not Popeye's 'girlfriend.' I see her as a real *femme fatale*," the actress said.

Duvall, who as a child was teasingly called "Olive Oyl" because of her tall, lean body, found that getting into her outfit transformed her. "Once I got into the costume and the wig, I was Olive. The shoes dictated the way I walked. They were a size fourteen and I wear a seven. They made me take a longer stride and walk flat-footed and it was perfect. Olive has her own kind of grace. I think of her as a combination of Stan Laurel and Mae West."

In the beginning, everyone thought they had a pretty good piece of celluloid in the making. Ray Walston, upon returning to the States, said, "It's the best part I've had since *Damn Yankees*. Altman never compromised—even when working on the treacherous Mediterranean in scenes previously planned to film in a tank."

But as the months dragged on, everyone lost spirit. Robin remembered that when he was cast for the role he thought it was going to be his big break, as *Superman* had been for Christopher Reeve. Once the shooting started, it was hard not to be doubtful, until he finally found himself wondering when he could get the hell off this rock.

The water scenes mentioned by Walston were part of the film's finale—and of everyone's final disillusionment with the project. The action consisted of Popeye fighting not only the evil Bluto (who kidnapped both Olive and Sweet Pea) but also a monster octopus who decided that Olive would be a tasty morsel for lunch.

It was supposed to be a big, pull-out-the-stops scene, but just before they began to shoot it, Paramount called and told Altman that he was over his budget and had exactly one day to return to the States. Everyone was terribly disappointed because they thought the screen action would be enhanced with special effects—Popeye would tear through the water with his legs spinning like a tornado and smack the bothersome octopus into the stratosphere. Since the special effects crew had already left the island, this proved to be impossible.

Even the giant octopus wasn't a terribly terrific monster. Robin had assumed that since Disney had a half-partnership in the movie, they would construct a realistic model that could move its arms mechanically, blow bubbles, and make facial gestures. In reality, it was a huge hunk of rubber that sat there like . . . a huge hunk of rubber.

Shelley had to wrap herself in the tentacles and flop around trying to look as if she were being attacked. Instead of blasting the octopus into outer space, they blew it up, but on the movie screen the resolution of the fight was unclear to the audience.

Even songwriter Harry Nilsson became upset because out of the fourteen songs he had composed for the film, Altman chose only six. And they weren't even Nilsson's favorites.

Popeye wrapped on June 25, 1980 and was released in early December. The charity premiere (proceeds went to the Los Angeles Children's Museum) was so packed with celebrities that the *Los Angeles Herald-Examiner* printed nearly two full columns containing nothing but the attendant stars' names in its report of the event.

Robin stepped out of his limo resplendent in a top hat, white tie, and tails—complete with a spinach leaf boutonniere—and he gave Shelley Duvall a bouquet of the same vegetable. Sweethaven's harbor was recreated in the parking lot behind Mann's Chinese Theater; in a huge tent there was a Popeye-themed dinner including lots of spinach dishes; tabbouleh, Greek, and Italian salads (all dressed with olive oil, of course); a beer bar for Bluto's buddies; and mountains of hamburgers for Wimpy's friends. The tables were adorned with goldfish bowls and seashells holding sweet (pea) desserts. Robin entertained the guests with a little standup routine before everyone indulged in the goodies.

The celebs all adored the party but the critics didn't all adore the film. The decidedly mixed reviews included comments like: "*Popeye* is not a terrible movie but it is a keen disappointment, a sizeable squander of talent, a bad dream in which everything looks right but is in fact all wrong," wrote Kenneth Turan in *New West*."

"Williams gives it everything in a hard-working, conscientious, and self-effacing way. Submerging almost everything of himself and of Mork into the squint-eyed, mispronunskiating mumbler Popeye is meant to be," wrote the *Los Angeles Times*'s Charles Champlin.

L.A. Weekly made it their pick of the week and said that watching the movie is "like going to Disneyland."

"Altman's direction . . . lacks shape and focus and he seems to be working at cross-purposes to the comic book origins. . . ." said the *Hollywood Reporter*.

Us magazine said that "*Popeye* marks yet another setback for Williams."

Newsweek claimed, "Altman's game plan is daring," then added, "But Altman doesn't have the natural instincts of a cartoonist; he's always been an eavesdropper, preferring to view his subjects from a wary middle distance."

But critics do not a box office smash make—that takes people, lots and lots of people. After the $20 million-film opened, people did pour into the theaters in respectable numbers. After all, "people" includes the subcategory "children," and exasperated parents need places to take their bored little darlings after all the Christmas presents have lost their newness.

During its first three days the film brought in an "impressive" $6,310,520 in 901 theaters across the U.S. and Canada—despite the fact that it was released during the traditionally slow pre-Christmas weeks.

During the first six weeks that it was in theaters, *Popeye* earned a respectable $35 million domestically, and the international market looked promising. The film probably could have done better initially, but some theater owners were afraid to book it because they thought it was going to be a cartoon; others felt Altman was too artsy a director.

Evans decided even before the film was finished that he didn't ever want it sold to television, feeling that it would be a perennial. He may have been right: When it was re-released for Memorial Day weekend the following year, its profits passed the $60,000,000 gross mark. Once it was released on videocassette, parents began to rent it over and over again for their kids.

Years later, when Robin analyzed *Popeye,* he felt that he had "guts" and his performance had "depth," but that everyone had been struggling against a pretty stacked deck. "*Popeye* was a case of people expecting one thing and receiving another," he said. "People were expecting a big boffo musical and they got a fairy tale. Even I wanted more."

He was satisfied that children greatly enjoyed the film and recognized that they didn't go to see it with the preconceived ideas their parents had. But that first night, during the premiere, Bruce Johnson was sitting next to a star who wasn't glowing too brightly. "Robin wasn't too happy that night," he said.

Somehow something had short-circuited with that big, amazing, wonderful, elusive thing called success. Robin was beginning to have quite a few nights—and days—that weren't too happy either.

▪ 7 ▪

On Excesses and Temptations

IF ROBIN THOUGHT HE WAS HAVING TROUBLE WITH HIS fame, he soon learned that he hadn't seen nuthin' yet. Even this early in his career, Robin found out how quickly notoriety can become a double-edged sword, ready to cut you on either end.

Now that he was famous, unknown comics suddenly came out of the woodwork squawking that Robin's road to the top had included stepping on their backs and stealing their jokes. Some refused to work if he was in the audience, worrying that national exposure would ruin their best gags. One performer reportedly shoved Robin up against a wall, accused him of appropriating a joke, and hit him up for $300, which the star paid.

According to comedienne Ann Mchen: "Comics have been confronting him because when he first hit town he stole all his material. He took a little bit from here and a little bit from there and turned it into his own flavor."

Other local comics felt that the barbs directed at Robin were more like a case of jealousy of his skyrocket to superstardom than anything else. Los Angeles-based Claire Ryan defended Robin, saying, "He's not just sitting there and saying, 'Okay, I am going to take this or that.' " Ryan believed that Robin's crimes were really no worse than any other comic's, because every performer listens to other people's routines before subconsciously working over the material into something new.

On the other side of that double-edged sword were the awards being heaped on Robin. In December of 1978, he was honored as Entertainer of the Year and Rising Male Star of the Year by the American Guild of Variety Artists. A few days later the Hollywood Women's Press Club awarded him a Golden Apple for Male Discovery of the Year during *Mork and Mindy*'s first season. In January he received a Golden Globe Award for Best Television Actor (and after being handed the statue he turned to the audience and grabbed his crotch).

Happy to lend his name to worthy charitable organizations in the hope that he could help make the world a better place to live, Robin began showing up at openings and fund-raising events all over the country.

At a March of Dimes walkathon in San Francisco he helped raise over $1 million. He was photographed squeezed in between Cher and Tina Louise at a celebrity fashion show at the Beverly Wilshire Hotel to support solar energy, and a month later appeared with pals Henry Winkler and Paul-Michael Glaser at the opening of the Los Angeles Children's Museum. He was the honorary chairman of the Annual Topanga Days Country Fair, where he wandered through the weed-arranging exhibit, sampled the contestants' apple pies, acted as grand parade marshal, blew bubbles, and signed autographs. Frequently, he performed at a local children's hospital and worked for a charity that gives battered children the benefits of art therapy. He appeared in a benefit at Off-the-Wall for Cedar-Sinai's preschool children's diagnostic center. He remembered one day when he woke up, checked his calendar, and discovered that he had volunteered to appear at six different benefit functions.

Then there were the parties: A-list parties, A+-list parties, society parties, comedy parties, impromptu parties, and wild parties.

Once he said, "If it gets to be too much—too many cars, people pulling off my clothes, too much fan mail to answer in a lifetime, I'll just go back where I came from"—but deep inside he loved the adulation, the invitations. It seemed that he went everywhere and did everything.

By the end of 1979 paparazzi Ron Galella said Robin was the fifth-most-photographed person that year. As Robin later elaborated about that period: "It was just a madhouse. A time when you didn't want to stop. It got to the point where people said I'd go to the opening of an envelope."

Once Robin was spotted wearing street clothes at a pajama party at Flippers, a popular West Hollywood roller skating rink. When someone queried him if he was wearing his bedtime costume, he smiled and quipped, "No, no. I sleep in a two-piece outfit—my socks."

Valerie tried hard to keep up with her party-animal husband, but this chaotic pace just wasn't her style. What she wanted most of all was to dance, and spend quiet time at home enjoying the man she married. That got harder and harder to do as the months rolled by.

The couple always managed to eat dinner together on Mondays, because that was *Mork and Mindy*'s easiest rehearsal day. One perk of stardom was Robin's own trailer dressing room on the Paramount lot, so Valerie would often join him there for lunch, or pop in to whip him up a health shake concocted of bananas, fruit juices, protein powder, and brewer's yeast. Friday nights she'd stop by to watch the show's taping.

Both tried hard to hold onto the special feelings they had for each other. One woman who

Robin's meteoric rise to fame began in 1978 when he and Pam Dawber were cast in the title roles of the TV series *Mork and Mindy.* "Robin is a very attractive man," said Dawber. "Actually, he's a pixie . . . the gentlest man in the world, but he's so driven."

FRANK EDWARDS/FOTOS INTERNATIONAL.

FRANK EDWARDS/FOTOS INTERNATIONAL.

In 1979, Robin was awarded a Golden Globe Award for Best Television Actor in a Comedy or Musical Series for *Mork and Mindy.* The show was so popular that by its second season, an average of 53 million people were watching it weekly and the producers readily acknowledged that it was really "The Robin Williams Show."

Former Juilliard classmate and close friend Christopher Reeve presented Robin with the 1979 People's Choice Award. "Robin and I were both supposed to be Shakespearean actors. I ended up in a comic book (*Superman*) and he ended up on *Mork and Mindy*," Reeve said at the time.

FRANK EDWARDS/FOTOS INTERNATIONAL.

PAUL RONALD/PHOTOTEQUE.

For his role as Popeye, Robin had to constantly squint his right eye and speak in a gravelly "Liquid Wrench" voice, as he called it. He said that portraying the famous cartoon character was "like being asked to play Buddah."

PICTORIAL PARADE.

The part of T.S. Garp was harder for Robin than playing either Mork or Popeye because the role was far more dramatic and director George Roy Hill wouldn't let the comic improvise at all. In this shot, an embarrassed Garp stands by while his mother (Glenn Close, right) interviews a prostitute (Swoosie Kurtz) about love and lust for a book that becomes instrumental in starting the women's liberation movement.

After playing Mork, Popeye, and Garp, Robin wanted the part of a character with two names in a film no one had ever heard of. He got his wish—playing Donald Quinelle alongside veteran actor Walter Matthau in *The Survivors.*

PHOTOTEQUE.

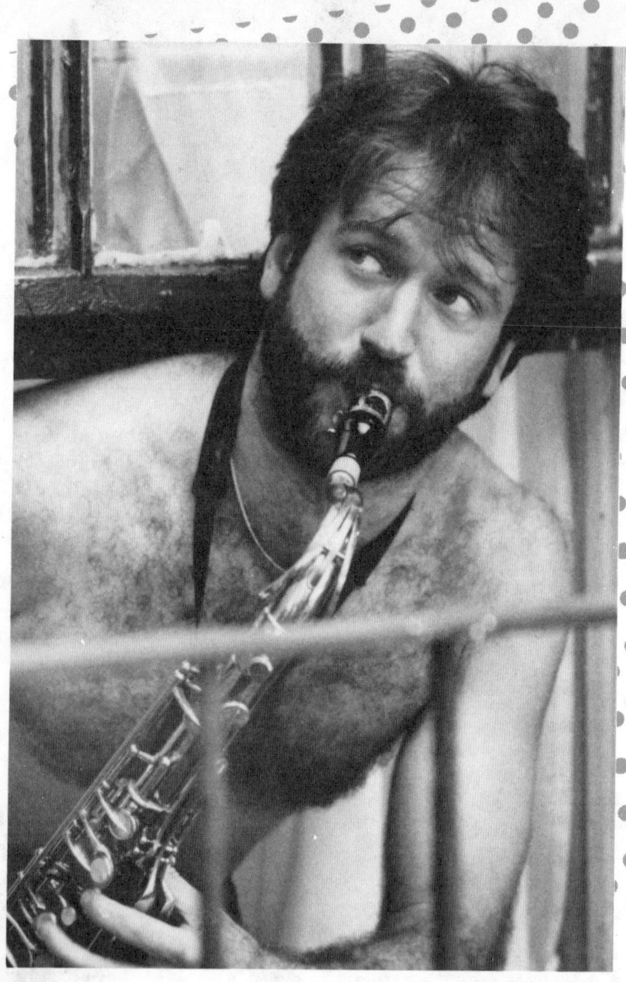

PHOTOTEQUE.

Robin grew a beard, learned how to play the saxophone, and took Russian language classes five hours a day for three months to prepare for his role in *Moscow on the Hudson*. He became so proficient in the language that the movie's Russian extras said he spoke like a native.

RON GALELLA.

Robin describes his mother, Laurie Williams (right), as, "always flying around, very bubbly and effervescent." From the time he was very young, she recited funny poems to him and told him racy jokes.

RON GALELLA.

The first time he laid eyes on Valerie Velardi, Robin said it was "lust at first sight. She looked ... hot. Caliente." They began living together a month after they met and were married a year and a half later.

DARLENE HAMMOND/PICTORIAL PARADE.

Robin may have thought something was fishy when he was named Man of the Year by ICAN Association (the Los Angeles Inter-Agency Council of Child Abuse and Neglect) in 1985. A true philanthropist, Robin donates much of his free time to charity work and performing at benefit functions.

A combination of his work and appearances in charity benefits — including "Comic Relief" — has brought Robin together with most of today's great comedians, including Dan Akyroyd (right), the late John Belushi, Whoopi Goldberg, Billy Crystal, and Robin's own personal hero — Jonathan Winters.

GREG DE GUIRE/CELEBRITY PHOTO.

ANTHONY SAVIGNANO/GALELLA, LTD.

Robin took a huge cut in pay when working on the PBS production of *Seize the Day* because of the film's "powerful, good script" and the chance to work with Nobel Prize winning author Saul Bellow.

JANET GOUGH/CELEBRITY PHOTO.

The birth of son Zachary in 1983 was the catalyst for Robin to mellow out and end his wild partying days. "The most precious times are those I spend with Zachary," said the proud papa.

ROSS MARINO.

Live performances are cathartic for Robin—a way to work out problems and anxieties without therapy. He loves doing standup comedy so much that he regularly pops into small clubs unannounced and works for free, just for the sheer joy of it. He describes standup as: "When it is working, it is like sex. It is complete freedom—things are coming with lightning speed, transitions just happen."

worked on the set of *Mork and Mindy* said, "One of the sexiest things I've ever seen is Robin running in slow motion to meet Valerie." He told everyone she was his "stabilizing force" and the only person who truly knew the real Robin.

The only time Robin and Valerie could really be alone together was on Sundays, when Robin became a complete zombie while recuperating from his exhausting schedule. At those times Valerie called him her "little autistic son. He's Little Andrew who has to be asked to pick up his clothes."

Bruce Johnson agreed that Robin kept a killer schedule in those days. "He was tired a lot and wired a lot, as much from his self-imposed schedule as from what his managers planned. Sometimes he would rehearse all day with us on Friday, doing two shows—one in the afternoon for dress and then the taping that evening—leave us at ten P.M., go to the Improv and do a full show, then he might drop into the Comedy Store for a while, then catch the last flight up to San Francisco and do one—and one time, two—clubs in San Francisco. Then he'd spend the weekend with friends and come back to L.A. Sunday night or Monday morning. Even when we were in Boulder, he'd find a club to work. Of course he'd work them all for nothing. He was at a workaholic state and loved audiences."

Part of Robin's crazed pace came from a deep

inner fear that the world's leaders would do the unthinkable—end the world in a blazing nuclear holocaust, or with some equally horrifying means such as germ warfare or poison gas. "That fear makes me want to create as much as possible before that happens—also, maybe try to have some influence on stopping it if I can," he said. He has hoped that through his comedy he can point out the scary way the world is progressing, and possibly influence people to think more seriously about the dire consequences that can arise from misguided actions.

As much as he wanted to help the world, Robin's frenetic pace was doing him a great deal of harm. Valerie became especially worried about her husband's health when she had to nurse him back to working condition after he suffered two virtual collapses from fatigue. Even retiring to bed at home wasn't terribly relaxing just then because their house was swarming with carpenters, electricians, and plumbers who were building an addition.

One of the luxuries they treated themselves to was a $2,000 Samadhi tank—an enclosed 8′ × 4′ × 4′ tub made from plywood and vinyl that is filled with salinated water and heated to body temperature. Its sensory-deprivation environment was the only place where Robin could finally escape some of the stress and strain he had put himself under. "You shut out the world; you totally relax in the tank," he claimed.

Around that time a reporter called to ask Valerie if she was intending to join Robin at an awards banquet that night, but she begged off, saying she'd already been to seven parties that week. She happened to add that she thought Robin was overdoing it as well. The next week the front page of a national tabloid featured a photo of Robin with a headline that read: "Too far too fast? His wife says, 'He's killing himself!' "

One time a photographer threw a glass of wine on her dress just to get her to react. After that Valerie was wary of reporters, but since Robin's career depended on publicity, neither of them could cut off the media completely.

One story that outraged the *Mork and Mindy* crew said that Robin had thrown a petulant fit that forced director Howard Storm to yell at him, whereupon Robin stalked off the set, delayed the show's production, and even threatened not to return for the next season. "I'll testify in court that the article is a pack of outrageous lies," an irate Storm said at the time. Robin was so upset over the allegations that he slapped the paper with a lawsuit.

Other problems with the press arose from Valerie's straightforward attitude. She and Robin would enter a party together and then go their separate ways, seeking conversation. People would ignore her until they discovered she wasn't plain old Valerie Velardi; she was *Mrs. Robin*

Williams. After realizing her exalted status, people suddenly became cozy and extremely friendly, making Valerie justifiably sick to her stomach.

Valerie began bowing out of parties. She hated the hypocrisy and catty undercurrents that flowed through all those blankly smiling Hollywood faces. Robin kidded that the local colleges should teach classes on how to attend entertainment-industry parties.

Valerie and Robin were both happier when she stayed home (except that she missed him), but other people couldn't quite accept that they were a liberated couple who didn't need to cling to each other constantly for fulfillment.

Part of the problem lay in the fact that Robin adores women, and they naturally adore him right back. He was always fondling and cuddling his wife, but also frequently grabbing at Pam Dawber or another female cast member. Party manners were no different.

Women thought he was so cuddly that they had a hard time keeping their hands off him. "He's so cute, every girl should have one," a fan once said. Some of the propositions he received would even make a seasoned New Orleans madam blush. One proper matron was overheard saying, "He's an innocent you'd like to seduce—and you could do so with a clear conscience because he's *not* really that innocent!"

As she stayed away more and more, the other

Hollywood women took it as a cue to move in closer and closer. And Robin didn't exactly beat them off with a club. Suddenly the tabloids were full of stories about his alleged philandering. He was seen squiring ex-model Molly Madden around town, and in one reported $2,500 shopping spree he bought himself leather pants and silk tee shirts before picking out a balloon skirt and top for her.

One *National Enquirer* story said that Valerie created a "wild, fist-swinging brawl" in a Manhattan disco after being outraged at Robin's open flirting with another woman. When cable TV hostess Nikki Haskell had offered Valerie a glass of champagne, someone bumped her, and the liquid slopped over onto Valerie's dress. Already steaming from Robin's lack of discretion, Valerie reportedly threw her own glass of champagne in Nikki's face and began punching her in the chest. Shelley Duvall was seen taking Valerie home while Robin stayed to make amends.

Valerie claimed that it was hard not to get jealous, but her love was for her husband Robin—the person. Most of the fans were attracted to Mork—the creation of a TV screen and the show business publicity machine.

She always knew that her husband was a free, rambunctious spirit. That's what she loved about him. She also knew that to try to contain him would mean squelching the spark that made him so unique. The bottom line was that Valerie had to put up with a lot more nonsense than she would have liked in order to keep her marriage intact. "If I had said, 'Don't cross this line,' he would have been long gone," she said.

Nothing he did was a secret to her, and though some of his actions wounded her greatly, she did her best to be strong in the face of adversity and keep her man by her side in the best way she knew how. "It was never any *one* woman, it was *lots* of women," she said, "and I'm not sure he had something intimately to do with them." Most of it, she explained, was just hanging out as friends—someone to have lunch or dinner with, someone to play goofy games with.

Never one to sit passively on the sidelines, Valerie made it a point to get to know women who were moving in a little too close to her husband. She would join them at parties, introducing herself as Valerie Williams, Robin's wife. She called them or went out to lunch with them and let it be known—in no uncertain terms—that her union with Robin was so strong he would never leave his wife for another woman.

Valerie had learned that it was better to guide someone than try to control them. She felt that by making herself into a vital and interesting person, by being important in her husband's life, she would bind Robin closer to her than she could with threats, recriminations, or ugly scenes.

By giving him the freedom to do what he wanted, she hoped he would overlook some of the easy temptations and excitement for something a lot more stable and meaningful.

At the time Robin explained the situation this way: "Valerie acknowledges my need to perform, and I acknowledge her need to dance. She accepts the fact that I finish a workday, and then still *need* to go perform at the Comedy Store."

Unfortunately, what Robin was doing at night was often more than just staying out late to perform at a club. The variety of wildly available temptations sometimes got to be more than Robin could resist. There were periods when he would disappear for several days at a time, never even bothering to call home and let Valerie know he was still alive.

"There was a period when he was being so disrespectful to me and treating himself to anything he damn well pleased. Instead of being a nagging, resentful bitch, I'd take vacations," Valerie said. One time she even went as far as Italy and stayed for more than a month.

Bruce Johnson felt that the root of the problems between Robin and Valerie stemmed from Robin's meteoric rise to national fame. "Three weeks after the show starts, Robin's on the cover of every magazine in the country, plus all the attendant stuff. It's got to be a strain on everybody.

"I've never seen fame happen that fast, and it can really only happen that fast with television because of the numbers of people who watch it, as opposed to movies which are slower. It was awesome the way he took off. Something like that will hurt all relationships. In a way it was too much, too fast. Robin was like a kid with all these toys in front of him. How could he not want to play with them? But nothing he ever did affected his work on the set, and that's a fact."

During this time Robin's excesses ran in many different directions. One was vodka and lime juice—ballooning his weight up thirty pounds. Another was developing a taste for a certain white powdery substance that makes you feel capable of doing anything, all the while not caring about any disturbing consequences. Robin's description of trying to go to sleep in a puddle of your own sweat with Buddy Rich beating out a solo inside your chest while every bird and animal knows you're screwed up inside was obviously drawn from personal experience.

"Cocaine—what a wonderful drug! Anything that makes you paranoid and impotent, mmmm, give me some of that!" Robin said, adding that the drug is definitely "God's way of saying you're making too much money."

Robin hadn't been a drug user in San Francisco—partly because he didn't have any discretionary income to throw around and partly because he hadn't found any reason to take anything that had no positive results. But cocaine . . . now that was something entirely different. At the beginning, it really was a pause that refreshed, especially after an eighteen-hour day.

Often called a "stimulus junkie" by his wife, Robin relished a supersonic pace. Life in the fast lane for this man meant the Concorde, not the freeway. He always wanted to do more, see more, go more, perform more, party more, and just more more.

Now that he was earning an incredible amount of money he found that drugs were always there, but he has insisted that he never worked high on cocaine. The one time he tried to, the stimulant actually slowed him down, preventing him from thinking clearly at the frenetic pace he enjoyed. It deadened his response time along with his nerves.

But friends have remembered a number of after-hours parties where the "snow" flowed in deep drifts. "I was there one night at the Comedy Store when Robin and Richard Pryor had just finished a set together," said one former employee of the club. "They sat together at a table backstage which had a huge pile of coke on it, generously offering toots to anyone who passed by."

It took several years of being what he called

an "asshole" before Robin finally realized what he was doing to himself and his marriage. He found that people will give stars drugs and other "goodies" to get control over them.

Although he has said that "cocaine is one of the most selfish drugs in the world—the world is as big as your nostril," throughout this whole crazy period Robin still retained much of his sweetness.

Paul Mirane, who worked as a grip on *Mork and Mindy*, remembered how Robin once asked him what he wanted for his upcoming birthday. "There wasn't really anything I needed, so I told him I wanted a bottle of 1973 Dom Perignon champagne. He chased all over town looking for it, and gave it to me that night at the Comedy Store. Then he and his friends stood there and roasted me. It was one of the funniest and best nights of my life."

Yet Robin continued to give in to temptations. He didn't really change his ways until he made his next movie. Luckily, its profound message showed him that a quiet family life really is all it's cracked up to be. After it was finished he and Valerie decided it was time to get the hell out of L.A. and start making a baby.

8

A New Life According to Robin

AFTER NEARLY DESTROYING *MORK* WITH STUPIDITY, ABC began making some quick changes in the hopes of getting the show back on its feet. First the network plunked the show back into its old time slot on Thursdays. Next, it decided to liven things up with a little T&A, or "tits'n'ass," as they're crassly known.

This T&A was something much more adult than trolls and angels, or toys and apples. Wide-eyed children were pointing out amazing things on the screen while horrified parents were quickly whisking them off to beddy-bye.

"It was pure T&A," Robin said. "ABC tried to turn us into *Charlie's Angels*, to exploit a lot of jiggly female flesh."

Pam Dawber agreed that the turn of events was "disgusting. We got a lot of mail asking what happened to the old *Mork and Mindy*."

One such two-part segment had Raquel Welch in the role of a curvaceous alien who subjects our hero to cruel and sensual tortures while she's dressed in a Bob Mackie costume that was hotter than Dante's inferno. One of Raquel's partners—*Playboy* Playmate Debra Jo Fondren—was supposed to put Mork into a hot tub and whip him with her long, braided blonde hair. Fortunately, the viewers were spared that bit of punishment.

Another time Mork decided to join the Denver Broncos cheerleaders, and photos of Robin dressed in drag ran in every newspaper in the country.

"The stories just got too complex and we got away from the simplicity of the character," Robin said. "Part of the show's charm was that Mork and Mindy were both very straitlaced . . . the show began with very human roots."

"Part of the downfall of the show was that it got a little weird," Bruce Johnson agreed sadly. "I am one of the people responsible for it from a negative side. The show had a sweetness in the first year and a half that was hard to retain. It just got a little strange. The T&A element came from ABC in its infinite wisdom, and we all hated that. They forced us to do the segment with Raquel Welch, and wanted the Denver Broncos show to be pure T&A but we tricked them and made it into a women's lib story.

"They [ABC] got real greedy. They moved the show to a different time slot and tried to build another evening, and the audience resented it."

Robin was particularly bothered by the changes in the show, and said, "I didn't want to see *Mork and Mindy* bastardized that way, but it was."

Even though his own nightclub routine is triple X-rated, Robin was extremely conscious of his young TV audience. He tried hard to present a wholesome program with a message that would teach without being preachy—something kids could enjoy but was still hip. That hipness, however, got him in trouble with the censors week after week.

"We had a tremendous problem with the censors," Johnson remembered. "ABC's censorship department is behind even the other two networks. Robin was so much faster and brighter than the censors that he could blow things by them using other languages and slang which was so hip they wouldn't even understand it. We had to do a certain amount of editing ourselves, to get rid of the things they would catch after viewing it two or three times. Our censor was the brightest and hippest; he really appreciated Robin's comedy and often put his job on the line fighting to keep some things in or just letting them pass by."

So the producers had a funny quandary on

their hands: The network wanted them to put on shows that were blatantly more sexy than they wanted to do, but at the same time would cut out double-entendres, slightly off-color jokes, or routines that might offend sponsors.

Robin once wanted to do a gag involving a fast-food stand selling kangaroo burgers: little patties with pockets in them, which held another tiny burger with a pocket holding another burger, and so on. ABC axed it because a big hamburger chain was one of *Mork*'s major sponsors.

"Another time I was going to talk about sugar and then go into a hypoglycemic fit," Robin said, but a candy-manufacturing sponsor nixed that routine.

Frustrated from the way *Mork* was heading as well as disappointed with his *Popeye* experience, Robin heard that a film version of *The World According to Garp* was in the planning stages. During the six months on Malta he had devoured the book, and knew in his soul that the role of T.S. Garp was made for him.

By April of 1978, John Irving's epic about a sensitive novelist born to an unmarried nurse-turned-author (who will write a book that practically starts the radical feminist movement) had spent twenty weeks on the hardcover bestseller list and twenty-six weeks on the paperback list, selling more than 110,000 and 3 million copies in the respective categories.

The first notices in the trade papers said that the movie would star Paul Newman, and Robert Redford would direct. Warner Brothers then approached George Roy Hill. He began reading the book, put it down as impossible after the first hundred pages, then picked it up again and decided to give it a shot.

Hill knew that such a complex book would need a damn good script. He turned first to William Goldman, who had previously worked with him on *Butch Cassidy and the Sundance Kid*, but the writer had problems visualizing the book as a movie. John Irving was next asked if he wanted the honors, but he felt too close to the work. After all, he'd already spent four years writing it. Nora Ephron also looked at the project and declined.

The next person Hill spoke to was Steve Tesich, because he had originally wanted to produce Tesich's Academy Award-winning *Breaking Away*.

Tesich said that writing the screenplay for *Garp* was like doing his autobiography—he'd been a wrestler who wanted to be a writer, and he also had a mother quite similar to Jenny. "I've always wanted to write something that encompassed a man's entire life from the cradle to the grave," he said.

When Robin heard that the film would be

made, he sought out the role, telling his agent to get him an audition with Hill. Robin was nervous about reading for the director. His popularity had already cooled off a bit, and this was the first dramatic role he was going to attempt. They met at the director's house in Malibu and after the first reading Hill told Robin he "had a certain quality" but he was speaking too rapidly.

Over and over Robin read the lines after repeatedly being told to slow down and relax. Hill, who had won an Oscar for *The Sting* and previously transformed another difficult book—*Slaughterhouse 5*—onto the screen, saw the potential in Robin and decided the actor was worth the work to get what he wanted.

Although he'd seen *Popeye* and one segment of *Mork*, Hill couldn't understand a word Robin said either time and thought of him mainly as a standup comic. Yet he intuitively felt that Robin had the same basic "underlying decency" so crucial to the role of Garp.

"I was attracted to his combination of toughness and gentleness," Hill said, defending his choice of Robin, a move many people in the movie industry thought was sheer lunacy. "Robin's an extraordinary talent. He's an actor, a real actor, not just a comedian who is put into a role requiring acting," the director added.

In Hill's opinion, Robin possessed the proper blend of comedy and reality for the part. Looking slightly older than his twenty-nine years was another plus because his role would begin when Garp was eighteen and finish at age thirty-four.

Since Hill knew exactly what he wanted, playing the role of Garp was much harder for Robin than either Mork or Popeye, where he had been given considerable freedom to improvise. Everything about shooting the two movies was completely different—especially the styles of the directors. "It was incredible to go from an Altman, who gives you all that freedom, to a Hill, who says, 'You've got to do it *this* way'; they're like the yin and yang of the directing school.

"Hill knows *exactly* what he wants. On the day we started shooting *Garp*, I improvised a line and Hill called a wrap for the set. I thought, 'Okay, you've made your point. I won't do *that* again.' "

Production on *Garp* began on April 10, 1981. Robin said it was hard for him to stick to playing a single character—and a serious, deep thinking one at that. He described the experience like: "drilling for oil. *Heavy*. But like comedy, to play it right, I had to relax. Not easy when we're dealing with one man's whole life."

Delving deep inside himself, he was forced to examine the raw emotions of family life—the love between a husband and wife during difficult situations such as adultery and the death of a son; the love of a man for his mother, the father he never knew, and his children; and the growth and change a man experiences in his life.

"My other stuff is more flighty and fancy," he said at the time. "Playing Garp is really stretching to go down to the sinews and open up your muscles."

Another difficult part of the role involved the wrestling scenes. Although he'd been a wrestling star in high school, that had been a long time ago. Now coached by author John Irving, who played the coach in the film, Robin found himself doing pretzel imitations for nine or ten hours a day. He built up his chest and forearms before rehearsals began, but wrestling with the film's teenagers was still a challenge.

In fact, the entire film was challenging, from the emotional and complex roles portrayed by the actors down to an incredible stunt with an airplane.

Picking an actor to play the role of Roberta Muldoon—the retired Philadelphia Eagles tight end who underwent an operation to become a woman—was no easy task. Hill and casting director Marion Dougherty considered using an actress, but they felt that the role really required a man to bring Roberta's rich tapestry of emotions to life.

Four screen tests were filmed, requiring different actors to throw a forward pass and receive a hike from center; answer spontaneous questions from Hill about the transsexual operation; and read a scene where Roberta complains to Garp about the hate mail she'd been receiving (including one hoping she'd get "gang-banged by the Oakland Raiders"). After all were viewed, John Lithgow was the unanimous choice, and the role will go down in history as one of his best screen portrayals.

Glenn Close was also worried about taking on the role of Garp's mother, Jenny. Previously, she had worked solely on the stage, and she said she was "frightened by the part at first." As if playing a woman who was at once rock hard and softly feminine wasn't difficult enough, Close would also have to age from twenty-five to fifty-eight in the film.

Both actors have insisted that Hill's marvelous direction was responsible for their stunning performances.

The film's interior scenes, designed by Academy Award-winner Henry Bumstead, were shot in an enormous warehouse of a soundstage, the Astoria, in Queens, New York. All of the interiors—the infirmary where Jenny impregnates herself on a quadriplegic fighter pilot, the rooms in Garp's house, the Greenwich Village apartment he shares with his mom as they both train to be writers, even the wrestling gymnasium—were set up inside.

Probably the wildest shot in the movie is when a plane crashes into a house Garp and his bride Helen (Mary Beth Hurt) are considering buying. A fake front of a house was built at Lincoln Park Airfield in New Jersey. After shearing off its wings on two telephone poles, the plane is supposed to crash into a patch of balsawood. The pilot had to maintain a constant speed of forty-eight to fifty miles-per-hour and hit the balsawood section right on target so the plane would catch in a net and rest with its tail sticking out of the wall.

The pilot, Jim Appleby, already stiff from a recent crackup in Nevada that had totaled a triplane and given him "minor injuries" (a broken back, eleven stitches over one eye, and a jaw that wouldn't move), hit the wall right on target. But then the plane slid inside the "house" and disappeared. Appleby was fine, but the crew had to pull the plane out and reshoot the end of the scene—where the pilot gets out of the plane, asks the people on the ground if they are okay, then totters off to borrow their phone—on another day.

Hill said that the hardest part of filming *Garp* was keeping all the fragments making up the story clear in his mind. "You lose sight of the overall plan until after you've finished shooting."

Because of the intensity of the emotions running through the film, Robin refused to watch any of the movie's dailies during the shooting. Acting in *Garp* felt "like drowning, like running for your life," he said. Some days he'd crawl back to his hotel so exhausted he felt like he was dying, and at other times he'd sit down and weep following some particularly touching scene.

During the ten weeks the crew was shooting in and around New York, Robin would sometimes zoom into Manhattan and perform in a club like Catch a Rising Star to release some of the pent-up emotions. Most nights, though, the strain of the role he was acting out made him incapable of doing anything after dinner except sleep.

During the filming Valerie was constantly by Robin's side. No longer working as a teacher but continuing to take dance classes, she provided him with the love and support he needed so badly after a long day on the set.

With her he had his safe harbor, a place where he could relax. There was no need to impress or entertain her. He could just be himself and she understood him completely. She stood solidly beside him, as she had through all the ups and downs, the good times on the top of the world and the crushing depressions. She continued to follow him to clubs and tape his act, all the time relishing this delightfully funny man. Later, she'd help him analyze his performance, what had worked, what hadn't, and why.

Although Robin was still drinking heavily at the time (he even refused to eat dinner at one *sushi* bar because they didn't serve *sake*), he began to realize just how much the jet-speed pace had been hurting their relationship.

He liked the Garp character, admiring the discipline necessary to be a writer. His lifelong dream of being an author suddenly resurfaced, and Robin tried to sit down and write, just to experience the feeling.

Robin felt that Garp came along at just the right time, and that he was terribly lucky to land the role. "It was like going from Marvel Comics to Tolstoy. Garp is like another side of me—the nonperforming side." It made him think seriously about acting, and took him back six years to recall his training at Juilliard.

The role of Garp also uncovered a little spark in Robin that he hadn't really known was locked up inside him—a profound love for children. Working with Wesley Ivan Hurt on *Popeye* had been whimsical and fun, but there was a touching reality to the relationship between Robin and the two children who played his sons in *Garp* (Nathan Babcock as Duncan and Ian MacGregor as Walt).

Nathan didn't come on the set with any preconceived notions about Robin, because he didn't have a television set in his house and had never seen *Mork*. Relating to him on a one-to-one basis and becoming close friends was probably the most meaningful experience Robin had while making the movie.

"After doing this movie, I want a family—real bad," he said when the shooting was done. "One really good thing about this film was tapping into that, working with all those children. . . ."

When *The World According to Garp* wrapped at the end of July in 1981, Robin and Valerie already had their bags packed for a trip to Europe. He needed to get away from everything familiar so he could think a little, become reacquainted with his wife, maybe even slow down and take a good hard look at where his life was going.

But the changes he needed to make were at least a year away. First, he'd have to deal with the untimely losses of three close friends.

■ 9 ■

A True Survivor

A LAST-DITCH ATTEMPT AT REVIVING *MORK AND MINDY'S* tumbling ratings came in the show's last year, when Robin's idol—Jonathan Winters—was brought on to play his son, Mirth. (On Ork the men give birth, and the baby starts out large and slowly shrinks down to nothingness—assured of having someone to lovingly care for it during old age.)

Winters had played a role in an earlier segment as the brother of another character, and Robin was so taken with working next to such a master comic that he would have gotten down on his knees and begged the powers-that-be to cast Winters as a regular. "For me, it was like the chance to play alongside Babe Ruth," he said. "I'd always wanted just to meet Winters."

The first time Winters saw Robin on the set he introduced himself as Willard Cespar, building-code inspector. Then the older man immediately launched into a routine where he was an old guard at the Paramount gate before segueing into a telethon attempting to keep Lucille Ball off the air.

Bruce Johnson said that working with Winters was definitely a high point of the series. "When we had Jonathan Winters on the show, the programs were great, but we all looked forward to the rehearsals and going out to lunch," he claimed. Robin and Winters "were so interesting when they were hanging out together. It was pure genius improv watching them and sometimes we'd try to turn a camera on them when they were warming up the audience. It was hard to get much because they were in front of the lights. Once the two of them got going we didn't want to stop them and couldn't even if we tried. They'd come out as all these amazing different characters. It was really special."

Johnson never failed to be amazed at Robin's improvisational talents. "Robin hits more than he misses, even more than Winters. I'd say that ninety percent of his stuff worked. Robin didn't improvise dialogue so much as *schtick*."

Although the ratings zoomed way up when Winters first came on the show, the writers still were trying to produce "promotable" stories rather than sticking to the simple fables the viewers tuned in to see. Once the stories became peculiar again, the viewers tuned out.

One day in the middle of February, someone casually asked Robin if he was aware that Harvey Lembeck had died. Thinking that this was a sick way for the cast to get back at him for all his own shenanigans, Robin laughed off the bad joke. He soon learned it wasn't a joke. His old comedy-workshop teacher, the crazy man who'd taught him so much about improvisation techniques, timing, and delivery had suffered a heart attack in his home on January 6, 1982, at the age of fifty-six.

A few weeks later Robin dropped by the Comedy Store where he did a thirty-minute routine at around one-thirty in the morning. After that he dropped by On the Rox, which had closed, but was told by one of the club's bouncers that John Belushi and Robert De Niro were looking for him. Even though it was nearly three A.M., Robin thought nothing of dropping by legendary party animal Belushi's $200-a-day bungalow at the Chateau Marmont Hotel on the Sunset Strip.

Robin and Belushi had met in 1979 but didn't really get to know each other until about four months before that night in 1982. During that brief period of time, the two found they had many friends and interests in common.

Belushi fell into the habit of dropping by the *Mork and Mindy* set. He was frequently in Hollywood because he was writing a movie called *Noble Rot* with mutual friend Don Novello (Father Guido Sarducci on *Saturday Night Live*). Belushi once sat alongside Robin, both of them completely enthralled watching Jonathan Winters work on a segment of the show. Belushi wouldn't even let anyone speak to him during Winters's banter.

Another time Robin went out nightclubbing with Belushi and watched in utter amazement as the big man played the drums for three hours straight.

"I respected him," Robin said. "He was a man who lived faster than any of us . . . a commando." He remembered one time when they hung out together all night. Although Robin was on his knees pleading for sleep by dawn, Belushi was still going strong. But a few months later, on Thursday, March 4, 1982, Belushi tried to go a little too strong, for a little too long.

He had come to Los Angeles from New York about two weeks before to work on *Noble Rot* and to discuss acting in a project called *The Joy of Sex*. During that time Belushi ran wild around town—taking massive amounts of various drugs, drinking heavily, hopping to clubs and parties, and putting in all-nighters working on his script. He was spending between $40,000 and $75,000 a month on all of his enterprises, and had a $1.85 million film deal in the works.

Accounts in the *Los Angeles Times* called the actor's last days "a nightmare of heavy drinking and drug ingestion." Former *Saturday Night Live* writer Nelson Lyon told the grand jury investigating Belushi's death how the portly comedian showed up at Lyon's house on March 2 with Cathy Evelyn Smith, a one-time backup singer for Hoyt Axton and occasional groupie, in tow.

Smith shot up both men at least six times during Belushi's last twenty-four hours with cocaine or cocaine mixed with heroin—"speedballs." The speedballs "rendered me into a walking zombie and made him vomit," Lyon said in courtroom transcripts.

Robin showed up at Belushi's suite soon after that round of indulgence had ended and found that neither Belushi nor De Niro were there. De Niro had dropped by earlier with Harry Dean Stanton, but was now indisposed. Lyon let Robin in and said Belushi would be back soon.

Robin glanced around Belushi's suite. The place was an absolute mess, littered with wine and champagne bottles; overflowing ashtrays; and crumpled sheets of paper spilling out of the trash onto the floor. He had expected to find a fun party, not a reeking, empty room.

Before long, John returned with Smith. Robin remembered feeling shocked that John was with such a hard-edged woman, and that he was a little frightened by the way she looked. For a short while he and Belushi discussed the screenplay the big man was writing about Napa and the wine industry. Since Robin and Valerie had just purchased a ranch there, Robin pointed it out on a large map Belushi had and told his friend to come up for vacation whenever he wanted.

Robin steadfastly maintained in most interviews that he merely drank a glass of wine that night and only stayed in the bungalow about fifteen minutes because Belushi looked so burnt-out. A later report of the incident by Cathy Evelyn Smith in the *National Enquirer* said that Robin and De Niro showed up looking for cocaine.

Bob Woodward, in *Wired*, his bestselling book on Belushi's life, maintained that Robin had a little coke, and was alarmed by the big man's behavior. At one point Belushi appeared to pass out for five seconds, then regained consciousness as if nothing had happened. Feeling terribly out of place, Robin soon left.

Robin has insisted that the real circumstances involving what happened that night have never been fully looked into. "No one will ever know [what went on that night], I don't think, because no one will ever open that whole bag," he has said. "If they do, they'll get into a whole other thing." Some kind of an undercover operation or setup, perhaps? Robin has said that he didn't know.

After Robin left, Belushi reportedly continued to guzzle wine and ingest coke, both by snorting and injecting it intravenously. Around 6:30 A.M. he took a shower and, saying he was cold, turned up the heat in bungalow number three. When Belushi went to bed around 8:00 A.M. he was "shaking and wheezing," according to the coroner's report.

After Smith ordered and ate a room-service breakfast, she was writing a letter in the living room at 9:30 when she heard "a loud wheezing" and rushed in to see if Belushi was okay. He woke up, said he was fine, and asked for a glass of water. After drinking it he went back to sleep. Forty-five minutes later, Smith checked on him, covered him with a blanket, then took off in the star's rented Mercedes to take care of some business.

After she returned later in the afternoon she called Lyon in a panic, sounding "intoxicated and very upset," telling him, "I came back and it was, you know, the place was—it was *Dragnet*."

Around 12:30 William Wallace, a physical therapist, had entered Belushi's room just before Smith's return and found the actor lying in bed, his clothes neatly folded and put away. Belushi was lying on his right side, in the fetal position, naked under a brown blanket.

After Wallace found he couldn't rouse Belushi, he summoned the hotel's security guard and gardener, Bruce Beckler. In vain, they attempted both cardiopulmonary and mouth-to-mouth resuscitation. They were too late—John Belushi had died two hours before from acute cocaine and heroin intoxication. Tragically, he was only thirty-three years old.

Shrugging off the *Enquirer*'s allegations (calling the tabloid a "paint-by-the-numbers" paper he often said he "despises"), Robin made himself available for police questioning and the subsequent grand-jury investigation into Belushi's death.

After the initial investigation Smith was allowed to go free, and she took off for Canada where she was later tracked down by two reporters from the *Enquirer* and paid $15,000 for her story of Belushi's final night. It was her admission in the story that she had administered the final shot, causing the actor's death; this admission led to the reopening of the case in July of 1982.

Robin was interviewed by the police in the Los Angeles offices of his attorney, Gerald Margolis, on July 16. Police would only say that Robin had been "very cooperative." The night before, Robin had been at the premiere of *Garp*, and when asked about the investigation he would only say, "I can't talk with you now about that, sir. I'm just so nervous."*

On September 28, Robin entered the grand-jury hearing and relayed everything he knew concerning his friend's death. Phillip Ryan, one of his lawyers, said, "Mr. Williams testified voluntarily without a subpoena. He is cooperating [by] providing information to the police department since early in July; he will continue to cooperate." Ryan went on to say that Robin was cooperating because he was "concerned by the fact that a professional colleague and a . . . friend of his had died and like any citizen [he] would come forward and provide whatever information he has. He's anxious to perform his duties as a citizen."

Both of Robin's attorneys declined to make any part of Robin's testimony public, and they also stated that the apparent inconsistencies between Robin's own statements and the *Enquirer* story were not worth commenting upon.

By Robin's own admission his career was at an all-time low. A *People* magazine poll of read-

---

* Ironically, the $100,000 raised by the *Garp* charity premiere was given to the Scott Newman Foundation, an antidrug organization named for Paul Newman's son who died in November, 1978 after an accidental overdose of alcohol and Valium.

ers placed him third on the list of most boring people—just under Carroll O'Connor and Erik Estrada. He realized that his residence in Los Angeles was soon to become history.

The period when Belushi died "was pretty much the bottom rung," Robin said. "You don't get much lower than that. It was a time to leave this unhappy watering hole—time not to wander down this canyon any longer."

After the season's filming for *Mork and Mindy* ended, Robin and Valerie went for some rest and relaxation at their ranch in Napa. The 600-acre property overlapped two county lines and bumped over hills and sank into fishing ponds. A two-and-a-half-mile dirt road wound past a security guard's shack off the main highway and ended up at a pleasant two-bedroom ranch house. Hawks soared lazily overhead, and the quiet was broken only by the furtive rustling of rabbits, mice, and deer in the brush, and the lowing of a herd of cattle. Robin and Valerie collected farm animals who wouldn't make it on any other farm: a cat with asthma, a sheep who thought he was a goat, a horse with an overbite, and another swaybacked nag.

Robin had first glimpsed the area in 1979 when he flew around in a helicopter before a March of Dimes walkathon. He remembered flying over a hill and catching sight of some land that was "incredible. I'll never forget that image—the colors, the beauty." He asked the pilot where they were and was told Napa. Then the pilot pointed out the local mental hospital and Robin thought, "Ahhh, how convenient."

The relaxing quiet of the area was energizing and invigorating. Robin could run for hours and never leave his own property, not even see another human being. "I call this my womb," he joked. "Womb with a view. Womb to move."

He loved the fact that the area was the total antithesis of the Hollywood social scene. Farmers would drop by and extol the virtues of their homemade wine and invite the Williamses to a tasting party sometime during the next month. Variety was the spice of life, not an industry bible.

Robin began carrying a business card listing his title as "Rancher," but since both he and his wife were vegetarians, neither could bear to think that "their" cows would be turned into Big Macs every year. Robin hesitated before giving the cattle cutesy names like "Chuck" and told people he was raising beef jerky—the animals would get so old they would just shrivel up and be sold as dried meat.

"It really bothered Robin that his cows would be sold to the market and slaughtered," said Paul Mirane, a grip on *Mork and Mindy*. "He used to tell friends that the animals were going away to summer camp."

On May 2, Robin received a call from his managers, but feeling the bad vibes in the air, he failed to return it. The next day he read in the papers about the demise of another friend—*Mork* had been canceled. Even though he had seen the writing on the wall, the loss still cut into him deeply. He once likened it to an old Lloyd Bridges movie where someone has his air hoses sliced by bad guys. The series had run for four years, and at the end Robin was earning $40,000 per episode, or more than $1 million a year.

Robin decided to deal with the resulting depression the way he usually did—he began performing standup comedy. This time he went on a grueling forty-day, twenty-five-city tour which he nicknamed "Das Bus" in honor of the vehicle where he felt like he spent all his time.

The reviews of the Das Bus tour should have lifted his spirits a little. "Robin Williams is a funny, funny man," said *Variety*. Paul Wilner of the *Los Angeles Herald-Examiner* said Robin "bounded across the stage with a mime's grace and an athlete's resolution . . . talents are literally bursting at being confined within his skin." Robin didn't touch the ongoing Belushi trial with a syllable, but he did work out some of his grief over *Mork*'s cancellation in his routines.

His show segued from celebrities doing odd commercial endorsements, to grabbing a photographer's camera and pushing it down his pants, to a trucker so hopped up on speed he wanted to drive his rig all the way to Japan . . . and it was received with cheers and ovations from capacity crowds.

Portions of it were turned into another comedy album, *Throbbing Python of Love,* then made into a special for HBO. *Python* also received a Grammy nomination, and the special was given an ACE Award nomination.

Other reviews appearing that summer must have also gratified him. *Garp* was hailed as a grand accomplishment for all who worked on it. Critics and audiences alike loved it.

The New York Times said: "If it was the book's whimsical side that endeared it to so many readers, the movie is missing none of that charm. If anything, it's got a little more." George Roy Hill's direction was called "capable" and Steve Tesich's screenplay was called "generally sensitive and economical." The title sequence of the baby bouncing up and down to the Beatles' *When I'm Sixty-Four* was called "inspired." Robin "makes a fond, playful father" but the critic felt that he was best in the role when engaged in some kind of action rather than merely standing still delivering lines.

Garp was a movie to "nourish" adults who were fed up seeing the likes of *E.T.* and *Diva,* according to Sheila Benson of the *Los Angeles*

Times. She called John Lithgow's portrayal of Roberta "tender," the film's technical details "superb. The choice of Robin Williams for Garp is only one example of the right-headedness of the project. Williams is sweetly randy. . . ."

But all the reviewers weren't falling over themselves with blandishments. *Newsweek* wrote: "A lot of people felt that *Garp* couldn't be made into a movie. A lot of people were right." The movie had so many disasters and heartrending scenes that David Ansen thought "the audience begins to feel like puppets on a string." He called Robin "problematic," adding, "his sweetness is contagious but when a scene demands real depth of passion, Williams comes up short."

Less than complimentary reviews aside, the film accomplished what Robin hoped it would—it gave his acting career a serious shot of adrenaline. Suddenly he was hot again, and besieged with scripts. *Mork* was definitely a thing of the past. Robin told a reporter: "I'm going to do a film one day that no one knows about. And I want to do one with two names!"

True to his word, his next film character did have two names—Donald Quinelle. And the film, *The Survivors*, was one nobody had heard anything about before it was released. Unfortunately, no one cared to hear very much about it after it was released. But what the heck—two out of three ain't bad . . . is it?

The Survivors also starred Walter Matthau in the role of Sonny Paluso. Robin played a nice, straight guy who gets fired from his job by a parrot, blows up Matthau's gas station (accidentally), and gets held up at gunpoint while sobbing over his lunch in a seedy diner. Together with Matthau—who just happens to be drowning his sorrows in lunch at the same time—Robin stops the holdup, but the two men catch sight of the robber's face. The gunman (played by Jerry Reed) comes to kill Matthau, but gets caught and hauled off to the police instead. Robin's paranoia builds up to such a fevered pitch that he immediately decides he needs to arm himself with a weapon for every occasion and attend survival training camp.

The film was about as funny as it sounds—not terribly. Although quite a few of director Michael Ritchie's ten films to date had been good (*The Bad News Bears, Semi-Tough, The Candidate*), something inexplicably went wrong this time.

Ritchie said he loved Michael Leeson's script and chose "probably the funniest man alive, Robin Williams, and probably the second funniest man alive, Walter Matthau" as his stars, figuring that the "yin and yang" contrast between the two men placed in a "vulnerable situation" would equal screen magic.

The snowy scenes at the Vermont survival

camp were actually shot at California's Lake Tahoe, because Vermont stubbornly refused to snow on cue. Ironically, a week after the company trekked west across the country, the largest blizzard of the year swept the East Coast.

Unfazed by shooting in the snow (Ritchie's career began in 1968 with *Downhill Racer*), the director found working with the sled dogs to be the most frustrating part of the film. Every time a shot was set up, the trainers would assure him that the dogs would run the way they were supposed to. When the call of "action" rang through the pine-tree-covered hills, however, the dogs would run in the opposite direction.

"Finally, we realized that when they were unleashed without a driver for the actual takes, they'd head right for the food trucks," Ritchie said. "So we turned the camera around, in the same direction as the food. It worked!"

During the production Jerry Reed suddenly became ill, and was nearly asphyxiated in his trailer. A subsequent article in the *Enquirer* erroneously reported that Robin singlehandedly came to save him, but Robin's managers were happy that the paper finally had something good to say about the comic.

The Survivors lived and died rather quickly. The reviews after its release in June of 1983 weren't bad, but then the movie wasn't either. It just wasn't wonderful, and in these times where people are bombarded with infinite choices of film, video, and live entertainment, a movie has to be spectacular to do well at the box office.

The *Los Angeles Times* said the film "does not so much disappoint our hopes as dissipate them. Both actors are at the top of their form, but the comic premise of the first fifteen minutes begins to come apart."

The *New Yorker* said the movie "may be too unpredictable for some people. There's a lot of unconventional humor in the writing." The magazine also acknowledged that it was an adult comedy, which many people would have a hard time handling since comedy in Hollywood's lexicon is generally the equivalent of sex-crazed teenagers ditching school on Friday to get an early start on a party-hearty weekend.

Robin, who had said after *Mork and Mindy*'s demise that he intended to take a year off but had ended up working on *The Survivors* the following winter, seemed unperturbed by the film's lackluster reception. He commented: "It was worth doing just to work with Walter Matthau—just to hang out with this man, an *amazing* human being. I learned from him, and I've got a lot of that still to do.

"We improvised, but no matter what I did or how much I projected, Walter would always top me. Every time he got the best of it by simply giving a deadpan look or by raising an eyebrow a quarter of an inch. That's really comedy.

"After *Garp* I wanted to do a far-out comedy, and *The Survivors* certainly qualified. I loved the bizarreness of the script and its basic premise of everybody sticking together during tough times. I believe things can work out—that's why I still perform comedy. Hopefully people will laugh and things won't seem so bad."

He thought Walter Matthau had been "great" but the film failed because the story was "so strange. I think people didn't care about the characters after the first fifteen or twenty minutes. It just got crazy. It's another film where we're struggling for the ending, at the end."

But right around that time Robin had something much more precious to occupy his thoughts, talents, and time. Right in the midst of the grand-jury investigation into John Belushi's accidental overdose, Valerie went to her doctor and came home with some news that made Robin jump for joy. He was going to be a father.

▪ 10 ▪

Saxy Robin

THIS WAS IT, THE MOMENT VALERIE AND ROBIN HAD been waiting for. The nine months of gloriously nervous anticipation filled with class after class of watching birthing films, learning the proper ways to breathe, when to push, what to expect from labor, and how to keep calm were finally at an end.

On April 11, 1983, Valerie was rolled into the delivery room of a San Francisco hospital, panting on cue. Sweat dripping down his forehead, Robin was clutching her hand and timing her labor pains. When the doctor hooked her up to the fetal monitor he discovered that the umbilical cord was wrapped around the baby, preventing any chance of a safe natural delivery. A little tent was erected and Valerie was given an epidural, a spinal anesthetic, so she was awake yet free of pain during the actual surgery.

After the cesarean section, the doctor held up the baby, who looked startled at being dragged out of his nice, safe, warm mother. He screwed up his face to cry and proceeded to wet the doctor. Robin found himself wiping away tears of joy. That tiny little pink creature nestled in his arms was his very own son. Hello, Zachary.

The responsibility was overwhelming—this mini-human depended on them for everything. Any last shreds of wild and crazy living completely vanished from Robin's behavior when Zach was born. "He keeps me grounded a bit," Robin said. "He has that look in his eyes, like, 'Oh father, must you do that?' "

Robin quit everything. No drugs, no alcohol —no more Jack Daniels, beer, or even wine. "I don't even drink the wine we make from our grapes—that's like being on a diet in a deli," he said.

"A kid forces you to do that," he explained. "You suddenly have a malleable little creature that picks up everything you do. If you are not together, he'll notice it very quickly. I don't get too manic or crazy around him. I've learned that I can turn off the voices very easily. It's becoming more comfortable to stay a few more seconds as myself so that he recognizes one voice as the 'basic Daddy voice.'

"Besides, you don't need drugs when you have

a kid. You're awake and paranoid anyway. Who needs anything else?"

Once the drinking and drugs were banished, Robin slowly began to get back in shape. His bloated appearance and haggard look disappeared with the thirty pounds he lost. Now a healthy diet—not broken corpuscles—brought roses to his cheeks. He resumed running, slowly building himself back up, and before long was trekking six miles a day. Taking some time off from work to be with Valerie and the baby, he spent much of it reading and playing games on his computer and searching through the various information services he'd been hooked into.

While looking for interesting work, Robin discovered that he was one of a group of actor/comics who get the same movie scripts passed around between them. "It's hard to find movies I want to do," he said. "I'm usually third string behind Eddie [Murphy], Bill [Murray], or Steve [Martin], and sometimes Chevy [Chase]. Much of it isn't for me."

But every once in a while, a script comes along that *is* right for him alone, a perfect kid-glove kind of a role. Vladimir Ivanoff, the hero of *Moscow on the Hudson,* was just the kind of character Robin had been looking for.

Robin, however, wasn't the first choice for the role; Mikhail Baryshnikov was the person director Paul Mazursky wanted. The dancer turned it down because at the time he had no interest in acting in a film about a defector. (Ironically enough, he would do a superb job on a similar role a few years later in the film *White Nights.*) Dustin Hoffman* was asked next, and after he declined Mazursky remembered seeing Robin using a Russian accent in a TV skit.

Mazursky said later that his final choice of Robin was an easy one to make. "There's not a long list if you decide to go with somebody who's thirty to thirty-five, with a sense of humor, who can act, and is willing to learn Russian."

Robin was delighted that Mazursky thought of him—he *wanted* this part. Even Mazursky's warning that he would have to learn to speak Russian didn't faze the comic. Deciding to make this his best movie yet, Robin began working harder than ever before to prepare for this role.

He immediately stopped shaving so he'd grow a good, full Russian beard. Then he began taking Russian lessons in San Francisco five hours a day, every day for three months. "It was just like a Berlitz course," he said. "I learned how to write it and I learned how to read it. My teacher, David Gomburg, was a director in Russia, and

---

*Robin has joked that if Dustin Hoffman has any more film roles he doesn't want, he should feel free to toss them Robin's way.

he was always on the set, and he'd help me get back into the language or the accent if I started to fall out of it."

The subtleties of the language fascinated him, and he enjoyed learning how to make sounds that are nonexistent in English. "My real problem was learning to master a Moscow accent, which is clean and crisp, as different from a Georgian accent as a Brooklyn accent is from a Southern drawl. . . . It was wonderful working in another language. It forces you to really be exact about what you want and what you need."

By the time filming began Robin was gratified to hear the Russian extras say he was so good he sounded like a real Russian, or at least a Czech or a Pole.

Mazursky had made a pact with Robin to learn the difficult language at the same time, but couldn't uphold his end. Even though he had a translator with him when directing, Mazursky confessed that he felt "a little helpless." He'd ask his translator if the actors were saying what he wanted them to, setting off arguments between the translator and Robin's teacher about Russian semantics.

The hardest aspect of preparing to play Vladimir wasn't the difficulty of the Russian language or the cultural differences Robin would have to portray—it was learning how to play the saxophone.

Vladimir, a member of a Russian circus band, comes to America on a cultural-exchange mission and ends up impulsively defecting in Manhattan's Bloomingdale's department store. A young black security guard (Clevant Derricks, winner of a Tony award for the play *Dream Girls*, in his film debut) saves him and ends up bringing him home to his family's tiny apartment where one more mouth (even if it is non-English-speaking) is barely noticed. Little by little Vlad gets accustomed to our strange capitalistic ways and even falls in love with another immigrant (Maria Conchita Alonso).

"[The saxophone] is a very sexy instrument," Robin said, "but if you don't play well, you sound like a whale having a bowel movement."

For about eight months before the filming began Robin took daily two-hour lessons from Greg Phillips in San Francisco. "I started out awful but I got to be okay," he said.

When he was practicing at the ranch, Robin would play up in the hills far from the house so he wouldn't scare baby Zach. He was actually fingering and playing during the filming, but since he was such a novice, his notes were overdubbed on the soundtrack.

The arrestingly authentic-looking Moscow scenes (complete with subtitles), were actually filmed in Munich's Bavaria Studios. Mazursky found that the standing street set there—Bergmanstrasse, created by Ingmar Bergman for his film *The Serpent's Egg*—was far superior to other locations he'd seen, including Helsinki, the site of *Gorky Park*.

Drifts of artificial snow were spread through the streets, and dozens of extras who were bundled into thick winter coats hugged themselves and stamped their feet against the "cold," all the while wearing bathing suits underneath the layers as well as sweating buckets from the eighty-five-degree summer weather.

"I've never seen an American movie that, in my opinion, showed Russia as it really is," Mazursky said, explaining the degree of realism captured in his film. "So I determined that this one would. I spent some time in Russia with [cowriter] Leon Capetanos, and we took lots of photographs which we used to duplicate scenes when we got to the Munich studios."

Having first been an actor (and still playing cameos and bit parts in many movies, including his own), Mazursky is truly an actor's director. He's pleased when actors respond well to him and feels most directors don't understand at all what the people on the other side of the camera are going through.

Although he directed the Russian actors with the help of a translator, whenever something happened that particularly pleased him he would simply say, "Fabulous!" By the end of the filming in Munich, all the Russians would shout the word whenever they felt something spectacular had just occurred.

As a director Mazursky refuses to fall into the all-too-seductive traps of making commercial films or sequels of his own successes, so his films are erratic—they're either brilliant or so-so. *An Unmarried Woman* and *Harry and Tonto* fall into the first category, while *The Tempest* and *Alex in Wonderland* seem to be part of the second. *Moscow on the Hudson*, by nearly everyone's standards, was an outstanding entry into brilliance.

Of course, Robin's precision and attention to detail while attacking his role was partly what made *Moscow* such a stunning success. After studying Russian and the saxophone, Robin began learning about the lives of New York's immigrant population, especially the Russians.

He met several times with Vlad West, a real-life sax-playing Russian immigrant. West lived in a small walkup apartment in the East Village, which was actually used as a model for Robin's apartment in the film (even down to the American-flag shower curtain).

"Vlad is a real, quiet, genteel man, very reserved," Robin said. The Russian detailed his difficult life in the Soviet Union, even describing how he had to stuff his sax with towels or place it into the armoire to practice, because if he made too much noise he could have lost his apartment in Moscow.

Robin's portrayal of Vlad was based in part on his conversations with West, his Russian teacher, and chats with the Russian-born extras. The rest came from himself.

"I worked harder on it than I ever worked on a film," he claimed. "I would prepare for every scene the night before so that when I came in to do it, I came in ready."

One way he did that was to pay careful attention to what part of the story they would be filming the next day, which enabled him to keep track of the changes Vlad was slowly going through as he grew to know his new country. "I tried to keep the subtleties in that transition intact so he doesn't get too American too soon—and too hip too soon," Robin explained.

To maintain Vlad's character, Robin forced himself to be somewhat isolated from the rest of the cast. He couldn't be a broken-down Soviet citizen constantly afraid of the KGB one minute, and then suddenly turn into a "Let's go grab a pizza for lunch" regular guy the next.

He found that the lives of many immigrants are not happy ones. "There are poets, physicists, scientists, and musicians coming here and having to take crappy jobs," he said. One poet he met in the Big Apple was so unhappy working as a cab driver that he wanted to return to Russia.

When the story shifted to New York, Robin had fun having his Bloomingdale's cherry popped. Somehow, in all the times he visited the city and in the years he studied at Juilliard, he'd never once set sneaker into the famous department store. "It's such a surreal place," he commented. "All those mirrors. It's like a car wash designed by Gucci."

Mazursky diligently portrayed the wonderful ethnic mix that makes up New York. Vlad falls in love with an Italian saleswoman at Bloomie's (played by a native Venezuelan actress); his immigration lawyer is Cuban (played by an Argentine-born actor); a Jamaican INS official interviews him; and after poor Vlad faints from seeing all the brands of coffee in a supermarket, he's seen by a Philippine nurse and a doctor from India.

"If you come to New York from another country I think you'd be shocked—not in a bad way—at how ethnic it really is," Mazursky explained. "All the colors and types would seem extremely exotic compared with what you were used to."

Struggling with unions and regulations to attain just the right rainbow mix he wanted, Mazursky was especially careful when arranging the extras for the scene where a group of immigrants, including Vlad, are sworn in as citizens.

"I arranged them so the 'best' faces—the most vivid—were prominent," he said. The people included an Asian couple, blacks, Latinos, Indians, and middle Europeans. Mazursky also specifically chose a black judge to reinforce the multihued American theme.

By the end of November the film was wrapped. Everyone felt pleased with their efforts.

"For me, the movie was a wonderful experience," Robin said. "Like *Garp*, I got to play a man whose life is changing. Not as much time is covered; the time is very condensed, but it is the story of the Americanization of an immigrant learning to deal with his place."

Now all that was left was to wait for the film to open the following April.

The day *Moscow on the Hudson* opened, one-year-old Zach took his first tentative steps. "Like a wino on his way to a bottle," is how his doting poppa described the monumental event, declaring that the timing was a good omen.

He was right. The film was a success. Audiences laughed until tears streamed down their cheeks, then wrung out their hankies to dab at their eyes during the tender scenes. The *Hollywood Reporter* blared out a headline saying, "Robin Williams *Moscow* film performance best in his career." The review continued: "Williams's portrayal of the saxophonist Vladimir is inspired and remarkably restrained. . . . Surfacing in his sensitive portrayal is the anguish of an immigrant who still suffers pangs for his homeland."

According to *Variety*, "Directed by Paul Mazursky with his usual, unusual touches, *Moscow* would be in a lot of trouble without a superbly sensitive portrayal by Robin Williams of a gentle circus musician."

"The movie's triple-A asset is a low-key, easy-to-love, and generally flawless performance by Robin Williams . . . given his best big screen opportunity so far, Williams works wonders with it," wrote *Playboy*.

Joseph Bensoua of the *Evening Outlook* newspaper, said: "Ivanoff [is] played with a light touch of comedy and sorrow by Williams, who proves a worthwhile choice for the role (Russian accent and all). Williams . . . is one of the best, if not smartest, actors in the business today."

Reviewer Merrill Shindler said: "Paul Mazursky's latest movie is more an exercise in good acting than it is a piece of dramatic storytelling. In fact, were it not for Robin Williams's fine performance . . . this would be about as heavy as a lead *pirozhok*."

Well, you can't please 'em all. Other detractors claimed the movie was too patriotic. The Cannes Film Festival declined to show it, saying it was "too political."

Robin was quick to point out that most Americans began the same way as Vlad, but subsequent generations have forgotten that. The star also didn't feel that Mazursky was too hard on Russia, allowing that the director may have elaborated a little on the hardships found there to make an impact during the short time the film has to make that point. He went on to add that there are much worse things in Russia that weren't shown—including oppression, bureaucracy, and harassment.

Phillip Roth once described the particular type of culture shock experienced by Americans who visit the USSR (and vice versa) as: "In the West everything goes and nothing matters, while in the East nothing goes and everything matters."

Robin returned to the ranch to bounce his baby on his knee and smile for a while. Right now he had an awful lot to smile about. He could even make Zach the only Russian-speaking toddler in Napa, if he desired.

▪ 11 ▪

Hard Work and Trying Times

THE MAKING OF *MOSCOW ON THE HUDSON* HAD BEEN an international experience par excellence: location work in Germany and New York, working with actors from all over the world, mastering the Russian language. Robin's superb performance had propelled him into the ranks of respected actors.

One might think that following such a glorious act with a simple football story would be something of a comedown, but not for Robin. Jack Dundee, the part Robin played in *The Best of Times*, brought him right smack into the minds and hearts of Middle America. Despite the fact that the film's actual location is the town of Taft, California, the sentiments can easily be found in any small American city.

In his senior year of high school, Dundee is thrown what could be the winning pass in the biggest game of the year. Should he complete the play, Dundee will finally bring his team to a historical first—a victory against Taft's fiercest rival, nearby Bakersfield. But, bungler that he is, Dundee drops the ball and is remembered by everyone in town for the next thirteen years as the guy who lost the big game. His life as an executive at his father-in-law's bank is reasonably tolerable, but a bespectacled and wimpy Dundee wants to redeem himself. He finally contacts his old pal and quarterback Reno Hightower (Kurt Russell) about replaying the big game. Although they nearly lose their wives in the process, the two friends manage to get both old teams back together, then have a glorious moment turning back the clock and replaying history.

Making the $10.8 million film was a great time for Robin. He was delighted that the director, Roger Spottiswoode, gave him considerable free rein, and the star felt like this was the closest to a Frank Capra movie he'd seen in a long time.

"[Spottiswoode] allowed me to be very free, to do *me, my* madness, in the film," Robin said. "My character, though he's this sort of confined, obsessive little guy with glasses, has these wild flights of fantasy, and all these other wonderful characters to bounce off of."

Another highlight of the filming was doing

the game scenes with members of the United States Football team. However, even though he'd played the game briefly during high school, Robin never pretended to be a hotshot.

"I have no illusions that I'm some great athlete," he said. "Half of the movie was shooting the big game in the mud and I made sure to give the real football players respect. At five foot six and one hundred fifty-five pounds, there's no way I could play the game [the way they did]."

Filmed rather quickly between January 29 and April 17, 1985, *The Best of Times* was, unfortunately, another dip on his roller-coaster movie career.

Paul Attanasio, of *The Washington Post*, said: "Screenwriter Ron Shelton has constructed a stand-up-and-cheer machine, and while that machine works, it doesn't make you feel any better about being run through it."

New York magazine felt that "the premise . . . becomes tiresome within ten minutes and one watches uncomfortably as Robin Williams runs desperately through eight ways of acting the self-hating butterfingers."

Variety called it "a poorly executed, shamelessly manipulative redemption fable that, despite its shortcomings, manages a reasonably satisfying ending."

Gene Siskel's review in the *Chicago Tribune*

ran under the headline: "*Best of Times* Not the Best of Williams" and said that Robin "almost singlehandedly ruins what might have been, even with its predictable story, a sweet exercise in nostalgia and the fulfillment of boyhood dreams . . . because he never, ever enters his character of Jack Dundee." Siskel found Robin's off-the-cuff jokes and one-liners especially offensive; the critic felt they were more appropriate for the stage or late-night TV rather than in a movie.

Whether the audiences read the reviews or not is not known, but judging by the fact that the film wasn't out very long, some of the unfavorable word-of-mouth seems to have gotten around.

But Robin didn't let any of that bother him. "Everyone said it was predictable, and I said, 'Yeah, but I still love it.' " He called *The Best of Times* a "sweet film. Sometimes you make a decision just because you love something."

Immediately upon wrapping *The Best of Times*, Robin jumped into another film, what turned out to be a mediocre comedy called *Club Paradise.*

Despite the great deal of talent, time, and money combined on his films, so many of Robin's movies are dogs that he is the first to joke about the way most of them "play on double bills with *Heaven's Gate*."

Paradise was another movie that sounded fantastic on paper, had an impressive lineup of stars, and then flopped. Robin plays Jack Moniker, a burnt-out Chicago fireman who retires to a mythical Caribbean island after being injured in the line of duty. Feeling sorry for a reggae singer (Jimmy Cliff) who manages a rundown resort, Moniker invests his pension in the property and winds up fighting a redevelopment project, getting in trouble with the island's British consul (Peter O'Toole), and falling in love with the redeveloper's girlfriend (Twiggy). The plethora of comedians who costar as resort guests include Andrea Martin, Rick Moranis, Steve Kampmann, Joe Flaherty, Robin Duke, and Eugene Levy.

Called "*Animal House* goes Caribbean" by *The Wall Street Journal,* the film—cowritten by director Harold Ramis (*Ghostbusters*) and Brian Doyle-Murray—definitely has too many comedians desperately searching for a funny story. Rick Moranis said the movie was "Noel Coward meets Moe Howard," but the *Village Voice* thought it turned out to be "the Comic's Nightmare."

Robin's part was originally written for Doyle-Murray's big brother, Bill Murray, who—perhaps wisely—decided against doing it. When Robin was picked for the part he was pleased and "loved the *feel* of it, though it wasn't then right for my rhythms at all." He added that Murray is the type of person who sits back and reacts to things that happen to him. "The problem was to change it for me, to make it much more active."

Robin felt that the film gave him a chance to learn from working with an ensemble, and liked how the different cultures—American, Caribbean, British, and big business—were clashing. "Integrating us is a real gamble, but based on what's been taking place on the set, I think it's paying off," he said during the filming.

"In rehearsal, I warned Peter O'Toole I might do something different from what's in the script. He said, 'Dear boy, go ahead. This is a *bizarre* way to make a fortune.' And once, when I'd improvised a line, he said, 'Damn it, I wish I'd thought of that first.' "

In turn, Robin was impressed by O'Toole's physical abilities. After seeing the British actor pull up his pants, tie his necktie, and smoke a cigarette all at once, Robin couldn't help but wonder, "Who is this—Doug Henning?!"

Calling O'Toole a "sweet man," Robin admitted that he stood "in awe of him. I think he had a good time. He likes to play cricket, so every Sunday he'd go and play cricket with the Jamaicans." Cricket was described by Robin as a game incomprehensible to Americans. "It's like baseball on Valium."

The $16.2 million Warner Brothers film was shot on location in Port Antonio, Jamaica, between March 8 and July 24, 1985.

Zach, then a "strange little creature" of two years, came to visit his daddy on the set. "Leave him at home? Never. He changes from day to day. He's a wonder, a miracle," boasted the proud father. Crew members remembered Robin chasing him around the dining room one rainy day, both of them laughing their heads off, completely oblivious to anything outside their own world.

On another no-film day (there were several due to a general strike that swept the island during their time there), cast members laughed uproariously playing Trivial Pursuit when questions like "Who played the ax murderess on *Mork and Mindy?*" were drawn.

Sadly, the filming was touched by a tragedy: A member of the Jamaican Defense Force had completed a parachute landing in the ocean, gave the thumbs-up signal, then disappeared. Although he was being watched the entire time by another member of the Force in a helicopter, the parachutist was never found and it was feared that he had been attacked by a shark. Warner Brothers made a contribution to express their sorrow over the incident.

Reviews of Robin's performance were actually quite good—it was the movie itself that was panned.

"Williams doesn't seem entirely happy in this movie; he's grown beyond this dipsy-doodle stuff, but he's too smart to try and actually give a *performance* here. His most convincing moments are when he's livid," wrote Peter Rainer in the *Los Angeles Herald-Examiner.*

"*Paradise* is like one of those 'What's Wrong With This Picture' magazine cartoons. It grabs you for about five minutes until you spot all the out-of-whack things that arc wrong with this romantic resort . . . the story line drifts all over the place . . . and Williams's seemingly ad-lib patterings lose their bite," said Duane Byrge in the *Hollywood Reporter*.

"Not a good movie, but a pretty funny conglomeration of comic skits. . . . Williams supplies some good wisecracks, but he's not playing a character, he's just being Robin Williams standing around being funny," wrote *L.A. Weekly*.

According to *Boxoffice*, the movie grossed only $8 million during its first ten days in 1,200 theaters, and it didn't look like there was going to be an increase in ticket sales.

Never one to languish over a project's outcome, Robin next threw all his artistic talents into an extremely challenging and completely dramatic role in his first period piece, *Seize the Day*, written by Saul Bellow. This made-for-public-TV movie marked the first time that the prolific Bellow's work had been translated into film, despite a number of previous (and profitable) options.

The story, set in the mid-1950s, was also difficult to get going. "People said, 'It's gloomy, it's pessimistic, it's full of despair,' " said executive producer Robert Geller. He countered by saying, "It has a Marx Brothers antic texture. I think it's very comic."

Even Saul Bellow thought there was some humor in his story. "I do see it, in a way, as a comedy. It's very sad, but that doesn't prevent it from being comical, because it's so hopeless."

The sad hopelessness of the situation is what comes out most clearly on the screen. Robin plays Tommy Wilhelm, one of those poor dumb suckers who constantly gets shafted throughout his life. His wife kicks him out and turns his two sons against him. After he works for years to build up a good territory, his sales manager turns it over to another salesman. He finds a wonderful girl who loves him wholeheartedly, but he can't afford to marry her. Desperate for money, he gambles the remainder of his meager savings on the commodities market, which swiftly takes a nosedive. When he finally sucks in his pride and crawls to his wealthy physician father for help, dear old dad resolutely refuses to loan him as much as a penny or even give him a pat of love and sympathy on the shoulder.

Fascinated by the range of acting abilities required for the role as well as the chance to work with Bellow, Robin took the part even though his pay was a mere fraction of the colossal sums he had become used to receiving. In fact, Robin was so impressed to be working with Bellow that when they met, he reportedly asked the famous author if he was carrying his Nobel Prize with him.

Robin thought this was his toughest dramatic role to date and he greatly enjoyed the "powerful, good script. It was cathartic stuff, but not depressing. It's such powerful stuff; it's unrelenting. It brings me back to what I was doing when I was a student at Juilliard, which is why I wanted to try it, to get back into that."

However, despite the challenge the role offered, he added that "there were some days when you go home and look for a power tool. 'Honey, I'll be downstairs playing with the buzz saw.' This character makes Willie Loman look like Andrew Carnegie. He's like a hemophiliac working in a razor factory. Tommy is not the best-designed person to be a salesman or to be living in New York."

When the inevitable questions comparing Robin's father to Wilhelm's came up, the actor agreed that he and Robert Williams had not been extremely close when he was growing up, but his father was hardly a cold, unfeeling man who "withholds love and makes you feel like you're wearing fiberglass underwear. We went from *Great Performances* to *This Is Your Life.*"

In between takes he reverted to his usual comic self, breaking up the cast and crew with the crowd of lively characters spewing forth from his brain in all their various tongues. Once the cameras began rolling Robin would say, "Guess it's time to go back to twitching," and immediately melt back into the pitiful Wilhelm.

He delved into the part by turning his powerful combination of energy and ebullience inwards, similar to "a laser beam; you have to take the energy you see here and take it down. It's like the difference between hang gliding and oil drilling."

The show, which aired on Public Broadcasting's *Great Performances* series during the spring of 1987, was considered a dramatic masterpiece. The cast flawlessly maintained the fifties feeling, and Robin's portrayal of Wilhelm was shatteringly realistic.

Newsweek magazine's David Ansen said that Robin's "corrosive portrayal of a desperate, out-of-work salesman, rejected by his cold, success-worshiping father, is haunting in its pathos."

After finishing *Seize The Day* Robin jumped back on the charity bandwagon. He did a benefit for the Southern California Nuclear Freeze Voter, and warmed up the audience before Barbara Streisand's very, very, very exclusive $2,500-a-plate Democratic Party fundraising concert. In between he found time to record a TV spot advertising a 192-page picture book commemorating the Live Aid concert, and cohosted the Academy Awards ceremony.

During the spring of 1986 Robin devoted most of his time and energy to organizing and working on Comic Relief an all-comedy show designed to raise funds for the homeless in America. Together with cohosts Billy Crystal and Whoopi Goldberg, he gathered sixty of the greatest comics alive today, including Bette Midler, Harold Ramis, Howie Mandel, Gary Shandling, Sid Caesar, George Carlin, Carl Reiner, and Martin Mull.

"It's not just bag ladies and winos anymore," Crystal explained. "There are a lot of families on the streets." When he saw the vast numbers of mothers and children living in boxes in the doorways of New York, Crystal thought, "My God, how can this happen in America?"

Formerly on relief herself, Goldberg said, "For me, it's not [a] hip [cause] at all. I was a welfare mother. I could be a welfare mother again." She likened the project to "a hand across the street," rather than "a hand across the water," then added that she grew up without a father in Chelsea, New York, had previously worked in strip joints, as a beautician in a morgue, and as a bricklayer.

Robin, well aware of his privileged background, joked that one hardship in his family was sometimes going without Perrier water.

The three organizers held a press conference in a $1,000-a-day suite at New York's Pierre Hotel, where journalists were treated to snacks made of lobster and caviar. Despite this inconsistency with their project, the Comic Relief show was a resounding success. The original performance became a four-hour HBO program which brought in $4.2 million in viewer pledges and corporate contributions. The project's overhead of $1.65 million was covered by corporate pledges, so nearly all of the viewers' dollars would go directly as aid. An actual $2.6 million was distributed to projects to benefit the homeless.

"I'm especially happy that the money got out so quickly to those who need it," Robin said. "Unfortunately, the problem hasn't gone away." He predicted that there will be the need to raise more money soon.

When they presented New York's mayor Ed Koch with a check for $139,500 earmarked for the city's Health Care for the Homeless Project, Williams began doing an impression of President Reagan. "Well, Nancy and I believe the homeless are basically people between homes," he quipped.

That summer Robin tried out a large-scale project of his own that was an overwhelming success—he put on two spectacular shows at New York's Metropolitan Opera House. The performance was later turned into a one-hour program broadcast on HBO, and then released on a ninety-minute videocassette.

The live concert is, without a doubt, Robin at his finest. He zooms from rolling out as his own penis, to what its like to live with a hormone-crazed pregnant woman, to the horrors of drug use (and abuse), to the poetic justice in his father's laughter at the way his own son is now treating him.

Robin fine-tuned the show to its razor-sharp perfection beforehand by doing nearly thirty performances on the road. He did say that about 80 percent of the show was scripted, which resulted in the polished final product.

"This show was much more driven," he explained. "Because of the size of the Met, there wasn't a lot of interplay with the audience." While he thoroughly enjoyed playing in the vast arena, Robin wanted his next performances to be on a smaller scale and "much more freeform."

Robin has predicted that his next HBO comedy special won't be until 1989. "It's almost like a locust cycle—three years off and one year on. You have to sort of recuperate."

By November he was back in Los Angeles, accepting the Man of the Year award from ICAN (Inter-Agency Council of Child Abuse and Neglect). After Whoopi Goldberg presented him with the stylized statue, Robin took off the longest of its clear plastic spikes and began to prance around the stage, fencing like Douglas Fairbanks.

"Me getting an award," he said after calming down, "is like Barry Manilow getting one from *Soldier of Fortune* magazine. I'd like to thank you and thank you for being vertical for just a few minutes."

Newsweek magazine's David Ansen, in a 1986 cover story about the comic, said Robin's vast popularity doesn't come from his ability to tell funny jokes. "What Williams evokes in people is not simply laughter but a sense of *amazement* at the spectacle of a brain on constant spin cycle. Classic standup comics from Bob Hope to George Carlin to Jay Leno are stars, but Williams is a shooting star."

Robin has continued to keep up a frenetic working pace, despite his constant comments that he is going to slow down. He spent most of the spring of 1987 in Thailand filming *Good Morning, Vietnam* for Touchstone Films.

Starring as Adrian Cronauer, a military disc jockey, Robin spins disks and jokes and himself with a frenzy inside the control booth. There is a great deal of interplay between the straight officers who try to keep everything running by the book, and the enlisted men wondering why they are there in the first place.

The movie reminded Robin of *Mr. Roberts*, where the guys in the back ranks during a war end up experiencing simple frustrations like finding food. And he was pleased with the project because he felt it's the first film to showcase all of his talents. "It's really a stretch for me," he said. "The stuff on the radio I can kick out and do the closest I've done to standup, even though it's sitting down. There's also some great scenes that are character-funny—simple scenes talking to the Vietnamese cook."

In addition to the wonderment of working in beautiful Bangkok, Robin was pleased with the spontaneous direction of Barry Levinson (who has been nominated for Oscars for his *And Justice for All* and *Diner* screenplays, and also directed *The Natural* and *Young Sherlock Holmes*). "A lot of what Barry does, which makes him so good, is he lets a lot of the stuff happen," Robin said.

Levinson claimed that he attempted to "instill a certain amount of confidence in the actors," then give them their heads in some of the situations. If things go awry, he'll pull them back on course.

Robin loved the Thai people and the rich spirituality in their culture. One of his favorite spare-time activities was to visit the country's many temples and shrines. The melodic language also fascinated him. He called the kids "ling"—which means monkey—because they would always try to climb up his legs.

Probably the hardest part of working in Thailand was the oppressive heat. "Actually, a hundred and ten degrees is enjoyable," he joked. "It's like tap dancing in a microwave." For two or three weeks he was sweating nonstop until his body finally decided to slow everything down, and force him into living life at a distinctly different pace.

Back in the States after the film wrapped in July of 1987, Robin continued to zip back and forth between various benefits and appearances. Although he is frequently seen with his son, Valerie seems to be noticeably absent from his life. Reports say they've split up and she's living in San Francisco, possibly with friends.

In mid-1986 Robin acknowledged that his marriage was on the brink of collapse. "Things are rough," he said at that time. "Maybe that's why there's a certain vehemence in my show, and intensity. One of the foundations of your life is about to change and you're going, 'Yeah, let's play, ladies and gentlemen, let's have a *good time*!' "

Perhaps the long lonely separations when Robin was off somewhere on location drove a wedge between them. Or Valerie might have finally grown tired of "taking care of two children," as she once put it. Maybe Robin found that resisting the temptation of other women was more than he could handle on a regular basis.

Whatever the situation is, Robin is keeping it private.

Though he has said he's happy, one can sense the pain behind his crinkling eyes, freckles, cropped sandy hair, and twisted grin. He's lost the impish look from the *Mork* days, yet night after night he has continued to give audiences that good time both he and they crave. Perhaps it is the most effective way for him to mask his own pain and sorrow.

He has said that he is trying very hard to remain calm and not overreact to the situation. During live performances he'll avoid bantering with the audience too much from fear that he'll snap and bark out something vicious.

Digging out the truth from Robin during interviews has always been hard because he refuses to stay on any one subject for long. After a straight line or two, he usually tells jokes with machine-gun rapidity, switching thoughts and accents so furiously that reporters forget what they wanted to ask him in the first place. He takes control of their senses with his humor, using it as a weapon to render them into helpless piles of mirth, writhing at his feet, all thoughts of pursuing an intelligent conversation vanished for good.

What about the future? Despite Robin's jokes about his agents not returning his calls due to the poor reception of his movies, fans can be certain they'll see him in at least one more film. But judging from the comic's enormous popularity and boundless talents, he should be cast in future projects for years to come.

12

"Gooood Morning, Vietnam"

"GOODBYE, STRAIGHT-MAN STRAIGHTJACKET. *GOOD Morning, Vietnam*," proclaimed *Time* in January of 1988. Finally, incredibly, Robin Williams's riotous, out-of-control, what-is-that-how-do-I-do-it wit was on celluloid, booming across the country to audiences aching from laughter. It was a bittersweet laughter—mirth tinged with faint cultural memories of one of the most painful periods in recent American history.

Good Morning, Vietnam was the first comic look at Vietnam. It was a *M*A*S*H* of the Ho Chi Minh Trail, a side-splitter with dark undertones, and as far as everybody was concerned it was Robin's triumph—"a one-man Tet offensive," *Newsweek* called it.

Robin had found his role. The anarchic, irreverent Adrian Cronauer, an Armed Forces Radio deejay who saves hundreds of young servicemen from the loneliness of life in the war zone with his crazed early-morning outbursts of jokes and soul and rock'n'roll, was the perfect vehicle for a solo star like Williams. It gave him a dramatic context for his favorite standup comic role, except that instead of standing on a stage in front of a live audience, he was sitting down in a control booth, with the cameras rolling and director Barry Levinson watching in sheer amazement from the sidelines as the star let fly.

Jammed between the likes of James Brown, the Beach Boys, and "What a Wonderful World" (camera cuts to bombings and soldiers in the field), Robin's trigger-happy humor just kept coming. In lightning switches he went through everyone from Richard Nixon to an anticamouflage military fashion consultant—"Why not plaids and stripes?" he asks. "You know, you go in the jungle, make a statement. If you're going to fight, CLASH!"—to Walter Cronkite, Elvis, and LBJ—who calles his daughter Lynda Bird because "Lynda Dog would be too cruel."

The potent mixture of sweet innocent fun and sharp biting wit that Robin had been perfecting over the years exposed all the tensions, all the raw nerves of those early war years in Vietnam, and made Cronauer a powerful, believable character.

It is 1965 in Saigon. Transferred from Crete, Cronauer finds himself in a sleepy, dusty town broadcasting on the morning shift to 50,000 homesick American soldiers engaged in "police action." By the time he is forced to leave five months later, 150,000 soldiers have been flown into Vietnam, Saigon is a place of horror, and Adrian Cronauer has become the hero of the troops and the scourge of the army brass.

Having begun by replacing his predecessor's syrupy Mantovani and dutiful news bulletins with Martha and the Vandellas and traffic reports of jacknifed water buffalo, Cronauer's innocence is quickly shot to pieces when he witnesses a Vietcong bomb attack on a bar and is banned by army brass from reporting it. His broadcasts become riots of irreverent sarcasm. They're uncontrolled hilarity, because the only other possibility is uncontrolled desperation. "Police action!" yells Cronauer, referring to the official term for the Vietnam war. "Sounds like a couple of cops in Brooklyn going, 'Oh, she looks pretty.' "

Robin as Cronauer is the voice of panic. It's almost as if he knew what it felt like to be in Vietnam in 1965, although in fact in 1965 Robin was a thirteen-year-old under siege by his school bullies. When he reached fighting age Robin was lucky. He got "a lottery number," a draft pick that was never called. Robin didn't know war, but he knew what it was like to live on the edge.

Cronauer was the perfect role for Robin, and Levinson was the ideal director for his unstoppable comic talent (he'd been nominated for the Oscar for his screenplays for *And Justice for All* and *Diner*). Levinson is also a kind of cinematic anarchist; he likes to let things happen. While the crew was setting up the main scenes for *Good Morning, Vietnam,* he kept a camera focused on the waiting extras, and then used the footage for montages throughout the movie. He shot all the war scenes in *Good Morning, Vietnam* with only six trucks, three helicopters, two gunboats, and a half-painted airliner— "Sometimes you can refine things so much they become less believable," he said.

In his search for the raw, Levinson likes actors to improvise. He had total confidence in Robin's ability to adlib not only the broadcast scenes, but some of the dramatic scenes too—including a scene where Cronauer jokes with a truckload of soldiers headed for combat, and scenes where he teaches "English" (how to say "you piss me off") to a class of Vietnamese civilians.

Although they had a fine script written by Mitch Markowitz, the writer repsonsible for several successful *M*A*S*H* episodes, Levinson only asked Robin to do one take with the script for the broadcast scenes. After that he left him free to take off, to go off the tracks, to make whatever wild and wicked connections he wanted.

Who else but Robin would have made the split-second links between the G.I.s finding themselves in Vietnam and Dorothy finding herself in the land of OZ("Oo-EE-oh, Ho Chi Minh!" chant the Wicked Witch's soldiers); between Oz's yellow brick road and the Ho Chi Minh Trail ("Follow the Ho Chi Minh Trail," sing the Munchkins; to the Wicked Witch as Hanoi Hannah).

Robin's broadcast scenes were pure, improvisational train of thought, the closest thing to a lone saxophonist blowing frenetic music on a solitary, late-night jam session. "I'm trying to do comedy like jazz," said Robin. "I'm trying to stay with things. I'm trying to get more of a jazz feel, more of a free form, where you can connect things up, like a jazz riff, like a scat riff, to the moment before. The object is to expand the time."

The broadcast scenes, which amount to about twenty minutes of movie time and a tangle of unused footage on the cutting-room floor, were shot in only seven days. When Levinson had finished editing the best takes, the broadcasts that theater audiences saw were pure Williams. The scripted takes just couldn't compare.

Levinson knew how to deal with Robin, who'd always been nervous of the cameras in his other movies. He helped the comedian by not saying when the cameras were rolling. Robin was always on anyway; the cameras merely came and went. "I could *ease* into a scene, and it helped me a lot. I started to relax," said Robin. Levinson also used a longer lens than usual, which meant that the cameras could be further away from the star, enabling him to shine, uninhibited by the machinery of moviemaking. "I just let him work," Levinson remarked.

It worked. *Good Morning, Vietnam* was the comedy smash of the winter of 1987–1988. In its first month on general release the movie grossed $53 million, despite the fact that audiences had to brave subzero temperatures and nasty weather. And suddenly Robin Williams was on everyone's lips again.

"Make no mistake about it: Mr. Williams's performance, though it's full of uproarious comedy, is the work of an accomplished actor. *Good Morning, Vietnam* is one man's tour de force," the *New York Times* said. "You may be all the way home before you realize you may have seen not just the comedy (and the comic performance) of the year, but just possibly the most insinuatingly truthful movie yet about Vietnam," said *Time*.

It was a breakthrough. Whatever anybody had said about *Popeye* or *Garp* or *Moscow on the Hudson*, as soon as they saw *Good Morning, Vietnam* they knew that Robin had previously been miscast. Robin knew it, too. "I've had an odd habit of choosing parts that were the opposite of me," he said, explaining that before, he'd always wanted to prove that he could act a straight part because he wanted to be more than a comedian.

Robin also said that as an actor he'd always been passive, by letting roles come to him. *Good Morning, Vietnam* was different. He found an early script for the movie on the desk of his manager, Larry Brezner, and immediately knew that it would be perfect for him. After that, the script was tailored to fit Robin's inimitable talent.

In fact, the idea for *Good Morning, Vietnam* had been knocking around since 1978. One of the film's producers, Ben Moses, had been in Vietnam in 1965 at the same time as the real Cronauer. The two became friends, and when Moses sublet Cronauer's New York apartment twelve years later, it occurred to him that the deejay who had coined the catchy slogan "Gooood morning, Vietnam" would make a good subject for a television comedy. Cronauer and Moses brainstormed and came up with a treatment, but at the time producers were horrified by the notion of a comedy about that war.

In 1983 the idea finally landed on Larry Brezner's desk, but ironically, though Brezner wanted to produce the film, he didn't think that his client, Robin Williams, was right for the part of Cronauer. If Robin hadn't chanced upon the script and seen his future in it he might still be where *The Best of Times* and *Club Paradise* had left him—in the great Hollywood dumpster.

At the end of 1987, at a party for the movie's cast and crew, Robin Williams met Adrian Cronauer, a forty-nine-year-old student of communications law at the University of Pennsylvania. ("He already looks like Judge Bork," Robin quipped.) "Robin was the me I would have liked to have been," said Cronauer, adding that though he did odd jokes and weird sound effects to the Armed Forces Radio formula, and though he was banned from reporting on the bombing of a Mekong River bar, he was never wild or outlandish like Robin. If he had been, he said, he would have been court-martialed.

By February of 1988 Robin was back home in San Francisco and back on top of the comedy food chain. There was talk of more movies, including another collaboration with Levinson called *Toys*, about the quirks of the toy industry. But Robin was taking a quick break after an exhausting press tour to promote *Good Morning, Vietnam*, a *Saturday Night Live* show, five comedy club sessions, and a guest appearance on Johnny Carson along with Bob Hope.

Robin had also accepted a Golden Globe award as 1987's best actor, and he'd been to London—not to visit the Queen, but for a performance at the Palladium in front of Prince Charles and Princess Diana in a benefit for the Prince's Trust; he reportedly had Charles in stitches over his joke about cricket being "baseball on valium."

Standing by Robin through all the excitement of success was a woman named Marsha Garces, "the one," Robin claimed, "who makes my heart sing."

He also said: "Sure I'm happy about the movie. But right now I'm moving through my personal life like a hemophiliac in a razor factory." 1987 had been a tough year for him, and though his professional life was soaring, his personal life was still in turmoil. He was trying to cope with the death of his father, the breakup of his marriage, and himself as a person.

Robin's father had died in October, at the age of eighty-one. He passed away peacefully in his sleep, at home in Tiburon, a San Francisco suburb. After Zachary's birth Robin had come to know the dark side of the man he used to call "Lord Posh," and he'd learned to love "the whole being," with all his weaknesses. Robert had been in chemotherapy; by the time he died he was a shadow of his former self.

Robert Williams's death brought the family together in a way that had never happened before. Robin, his mother, and his two half-brothers all gathered by the ocean in front of the house in Tiburon, and Robin poured the ashes out: "They're floating off into this mist, seagulls flying overhead. A truly serene moment," he remembered. He said his father's death was "sad, but also cathartic."

Robin's friends have said he is finally growing up. *Good Morning, Vietnam* was a sure sign of it—he's "taking on the whole human condition in his comedy," claimed one actress friend. Privately he is more introspective, more confident, and able to face his past mistakes—including his "addiction to women," which he now says he finds humiliating and degrading.

Robin has also learned that he doesn't have to be "on" for people to love him, that comedy needn't be his constant mask. In fact, five-year-old Zachary loves him most of all when he is just plain daddy. Being daddy, Robin claimed, is also teaching him to back off and give himself and those close to him a private space once in a while. "I never thought I would literally sit and watch a child sleep," he admitted.

Most of all, fatherhood is showing Robin that "most of your actions have consequences with the child," and this is the main source of Robin's pain. He wants to build a safe, secure world for his son, but right now it's a world fraught with tension. When Robin is touring, Zachary lives with Valerie. Otherwise he spends as much time as possible with Robin and Marsha.

Valerie and Robin hired Marsha as a live-in nanny when Zach was a baby—before that the petite and powerful young woman, of Finnish and Filipino descent, had trained as a painter and worked as a waitress. In 1986 Marsha became

Robin's personal assistant. Nobody's saying when the romance started, but Valerie is understandably bitter and angry, and worried that Marsha, who loves Zach dearly, will take her place in her son's heart.

Zachary is caught in the middle, and though a flexible shared custody arrangement was made in an out-of-court settlement, some tension is unavoidable. Like any other kid, Zachary can pick up on whatever is going on around him and will respond in all sorts of unpredictable ways.

Perhaps because he has such a zany father (and Superman Christopher Reeve as a godfather), Zach is one of those down-to-earth kids who likes a sane, quiet life. He does mathematical calculations "like a Jewish accountant," as Robin said. He prefers uncrowded restaurants where he can relax over his meal instead of loud, exciting places, and he thinks a room with a full refrigerator is much better than a camping adventure.

Despite his recent success, Robin lives a quieter and more measured life. He's trying to direct his energies towards his work and family—Zachary and Marsha. They live in an unpretentious garden apartment in San Francisco, and when Robin recently bought a new car it was a VW van, not a silver Mercedes.

Comedians are usually nighttime people, but kids are creatures of the day. When he's home,

Robin gets up in the morning and watches cartoons on TV with Zachary. Sometimes he and Marsha take him to Golden Gate Park, where Robin hangs out with the other parents and warns Zach of lurking dangers—like the older girl over there: "She can spell!"

When Robin performs, Marsha goes with him. They're in it together. She helps him figure out what works and what doesn't, and she has a way of separating the wheat from the chaff when it comes to friends and working relationships—something that has not been Robin's strong point. "She's his ground zero," one friend claimed.

When they were shooting *Good Morning, Vietnam* in Thailand, Marsha was "the hardest working person on the set," producer Mark Johnson said. She wasn't too shy to give Robin long, tender kisses between takes. Whereas Valerie used to keep her distance, trying not to step on her husband's toes, Marsha is always there for Robin, twenty-four hours a day. As his silent partner, she keeps his wildness in check. "I think I was crying out for someone to say, 'Enough,' " Robin said.

Robin doesn't discuss the possibility of divorce, or reconciliation. He's only talking about the short term now—the mere mention of future commitments seems to make him uneasy. And Valerie has said that she needs her own space to think for a while. "Neither of us were prepared for the sudden life shift," she said, "but I admit the other women were harder to take after I'd had a child." They're still trying to sort out their feelings. The main thing is that they realized they had to live separately for some time, "rather than to call each other an asshole every day," as Robin put it. He has admitted he's hard to live with. He has also said he's learned that his problem is a difficult combination of needing and rejecting love.

Robin has been learning about himself through therapy—"We're all in therapy . . . Jesus, I should get a discount," he joked. He never trusted in therapy before, perhaps because his mother, as a Christian Scientist, believed that everyone is capable of curing themselves. Robin has since claimed that it's "like having open-heart surgery in installments," and therapy has forced him to reexamine everything—his life, his relationships, his need to be liked. "It makes you face your limitations, what I can do and can't do," he said.

Part of it is accepting failures with his success. *Good Morning, Vietnam* has shown Robin that when it comes to comedy, and especially dark comedy, he's one of the best. He's a perfect clown, in the sense that his forté is finding a wry humor in the sad facts of life. When you can't change it, laugh about it. And that doesn't mean that he's not the actor he's always wanted to be. He just needs the right parts and the right directors; he's at his best when he can be free and funny. Underlying his humor is fear.

No one knew that *Good Morning, Vietnam* was going to be such a smash, and until it was, Robin was scared. If the movie didn't make it, he said, it would be no more than "a very expensive travel film." Another time he said, "If this isn't the right part, then there's nothing. I'll be doing game shows." Robin had been entertaining visions of saying: "Show me the vowels?" The joke was that as a post-Cronauer Armed Forces Radio deejay in Saigon, *Wheel of Fortune*'s Pat Sajak used to say, "Gooood morning, Vietnam!"

Robin has been thinking about writing his own script, and he also auditions for parts that interest him. It's always a sobering experience when the parts fall through: He read, for example, for the part of an accountant with the Mafia in *Midnight Run*, with Robert DeNiro and director Marty Brest. After three meetings and a close call they went with Charles Grodin instead.

But Robin has other projects. He's reportedly been working with Steve Martin, Lily Tomlin, and director Mike Nichols on a live performance of Samuel Beckett's play *Waiting for Godot*, scheduled for the fall of 1988 at New York's Lincoln Center. Larry Brezner, who as his manager has sometimes been a bit peeved about the projects

Robin took on, has admitted that this is one of his star's more intelligent choices.

Although Robin isn't ready to repeat his experience with network TV, there's always a possibility that he will continue to be seen on the small screen. He's interested in the possibilities of working in a series on cable, where he has the freedom to say what he wants—exactly the way he wants.

Another proposed pet project is working with his hero, Jonathan Winters. "Someone has an idea for us and a stage full of things—like a prop-house back room," he said. "Kind of like *My Dinner With André on Acid.*"

And of course there's always the standup act. Even after his huge box-office success, Robin still thrives on his late-night comedy club blitzes. He has been known to drive through the night streets of San Francisco, Marsha by his side, and pulling up outside one of his favorite old haunts. He'd wait quietly in a corner or outside until all the comics have done their acts, and then he'd take the stage to make his surprise attack. "Tammy Bakker's eyebrows will soon be declared a national forest," he'd snap in between a dazzling array of demented jokes and impersonations. Naturally, the audience would go crazy.

Whatever projects he chooses, there's no worry that Robin will ever resort to churning out the same old overused jokes and worn-out characters show after show.

"I have to try new things, because my greatest fear is of becoming mediocre, just falling back into the old rut and turning out the same old stuff without really finding anything new," he has confided. "That's also true for life—just trying not to get stuck." Many times during his club acts members of the audience will call out for old timers such as Grandpa Funk or Reverend Earnest. Robin always waves them off, stating that he'd rather try something different.

Sometimes Robin and Marsha go back to the Holy City Zoo, the smoky little club where years ago he tended bar and first met Valerie Valerdi. After his stint there it's back in the car and onto the next spot. If the hour is too late for San Francisco, Robin and Marsha might just catch the last flight to Los Angeles. Just because he's growing up and taking on the responsibility of a successful movie career doesn't mean that Robin is no longer a standup comic.

In any case, comedy addicts will be sure to get an occasional live laugh fix from Robin. He has repeatedly insisted that standup comedy is the only part of his work where he really comes alive. "It's like entering another world," he said. "It's such a release. Sometimes you realize that you've just said nothing. The nicest time of all is when the stuff comes from a place that you don't even know where it is. As it comes out you say, 'Damn, what is that?' "

The scariest thing for Robin is the same freedom that makes him so funny. "You're in control, but you're not. The characters are coming *through* you. . . . It's channeling with call-waiting," he has said. The fear is that the characters will stop coming. That's the fear that kept him living on the edge for so long. Now he's more centered ("Eventually I'll just be a dot," he has joked), and the characters are still coming. After watching his son Zachary playing with his rockets and whispering to himself in his different voices, Robin Williams would say, "That's where it comes from. That's the source."

Don't bother trying to analyze your gifts, Robin, just keep those routines coming. You may have started out as a scared little fat kid, joking to keep the bullies at bay, but you've become the best and most popular comedian in America. And will no doubt stay that way for many years to come.

FILMOGRAPHY

CAN I DO IT . . . 'TILL I NEED GLASSES?
(1976, 1979 rerelease/Dauntless Production)

Costars:	Jeff and Ernest
	Debra Klose
	Moose Carlson
	Walter Oklewicz
	Roger and Roger
Director:	I. Robert Levy

POPEYE
(1980/Paramount Pictures)

Costars:	Shelley Duvall
	Ray Walston
	Paul Dooley
	Paul L. Smith
	Richard Libertini
	Donald Moffat
	Wesley Ivan Hurt
Director:	Robert Altman
Video:	Paramount Home Video

THE WORLD ACCORDING TO GARP
(1982/Warner Brothers)

Costars:	Mary Beth Hurt
	Glenn Close
	John Lithgow
	Hume Cronyn
	Jessica Tandy
	Swoosie Kurtz
Director:	George Roy Hill
Video:	Warner Home Video

THE SURVIVORS
(1983/Delphi-Rastar-William Sackheim Production)

Costars:	Walter Matthau
	Jerry Reed
	James Wainwright
	Kristen Vigard
Director:	Michael Ritchie
Video:	RCA/Columbia Pictures Home Video

MOSCOW ON THE HUDSON
(1984/Columbia Pictures)

Costars:	Maria Conchita Alonso
	Cleavant Derricks
	Alejandro Rey
	Savely Kramarov
Director:	Paul Mazursky
Video:	RCA/Columbia Pictures Home Video

THE BEST OF TIMES
(1986/Universal)

Costars:	Kurt Russell
	Margaret Whitton
	Holly Palance
	Pamela Reed
	Donald Moffat
Director:	Roger Spottiswoode
Video:	Embassy Home Video

CLUB PARADISE
(1986/Warner Brothers)

Costars:	Peter O'Toole
	Rick Moranis
	Jimmy Cliff
	Twiggy
	Adolph Caesar
	Eugene Levy
	Joanna Cassidy

	Andrea Martin
	Brian Doyle-Murray
Director:	Harold Ramis
Video:	Warner Home Video

SEIZE THE DAY
(1987/PBS *Great Performances* series)

Costars:	Jerry Stiller
	Joseph Wiseman
	Glenne Headly
	Katherine Borowitz
	Tony Roberts
Director:	Fielder Cook
Video:	HBO/Cannon

GOOD MORNING, VIETNAM
(1988/Touchstone Films)

Costars:	Tung Thanh Tran
	Forest Whitaker
Director:	Barry Levinson

PERFORMANCE VIDEOS

AN EVENING WITH ROBIN WILLIAMS
(1982/Paramount Home Video)

ROBIN WILLIAMS LIVE!
(1986/Vestron Video)

COMEDY RECORD ALBUMS

REALITY, WHAT A CONCEPT
(1979/Casablanca)

THROBBING PYTHON OF LOVE
(1985/Casablanca)

ABOUT THE AUTHOR

Marianne Robin-Tani is a freelance journalist and author who has written for various magazines and newspapers including *USA Today* and the *Los Angeles Times.* Her first published biography was on Vanna White and her next one will be on Elizabeth Taylor. Robin-Tani lives in Venice, California, with her husband, Noriyasu, and cat, Velcro. She is working on a novel in her spare time.